UPSC

Syllabus for IAS Examination

Drishti Publications

(A Unit of VDK Publications Pvt. Ltd.)

641, First Floor, Dr. Mukherjee Nagar, Delhi-110009
Telephone: 011-47532596, 8750187501

E-mail: help@groupdrishti.in
Website: www.drishtiias.com

Title: UPSC Syllabus for IAS Examination

Editor: Team Drishti

First Edition: October 2023

Reprint Edition: April 2024

Price: ₹140/-

ISBN: 978-81-19544-89-9

Published by

VDK Publications Pvt. Ltd.

(Drishti Publications is a unit of VDK Publications Pvt. Ltd.)

641, First Floor,

Dr. Mukherjee Nagar,

Delhi – 110009

LEGAL DISCLAIMER

- The information, facts and news items published in this book have been thoroug examined and validated. If, by any chance, a discrepancy in any information or is found, the publisher, the editor or the book printer is in no way responsible for damage caused to any person or organization.
- We believe that the information provided in this book has been fundamentally writ by our content developers. In case of a copyright violation, the publisher would be held responsible under any circumstances.
- All legal disputes are subject to the Delhi jurisdiction only.
- ©Copyright: VDK Publications Pvt. Ltd., All Rights Reserved. The use, publicati translation or storage in a system where it can be reused or transferred in any form by any method (Electronic, Mechanical, Photo Copy, Recording or any other mea of any section published in this book, cannot be done without the prior permission the publisher.

- **Printed by:** Druck Media Private Limited, Greater Noida

From the Desk of the Editor-in-Chief

Dear Readers,

The Union Public Service Commission (UPSC) conducts the Civil Services Examination (CSE) to recruit the beautiful minds to the coveted civil services, the prominent among those being Indian Administrative Service (IAS), Indian Police Service (IPS) and Indian Foreign Service (IFS). The CSE is often termed as the toughest examination in the country. The standard and comprehensiveness of the examination requires meticulous preparation with proper planning, without which the aspirants of CSE are prone to fail. No wonder, lakhs of people appear in the examination every year and much more than this number prepare for the exam. Nevertheless, it must be noted that every year, out of those lakhs of CSE candidates, around 1000 are getting selected in the coveted list. So, the success in UPSC CSE is all about strategy, execution, dedication and perseverance.

A famous adage says, "It is our attitude at the beginning of a difficult task which, more than anything else, will affect its successful outcome." To put it in context, to prepare for the UPSC CSE, it is indispensable to have a winning attitude which depends on having the proper awareness about the needs and demands of the examination. There is no point in entering into a battle without arming ourself with the basic knowledge of the prospective spots from where our adversary will fire ammunitions. Thus, it makes it apt and appropriate to first know the syllabus of UPSC CSE before actually start preparing for it.

With this spirit, we, at Drishti, bring this booklet that comprises the syllabus of the UPSC CSE. Inter alia, the detailed syllabus of Optional subjects will also help you decide which Optional to choose. An aspirant is requested to go through this booklet to get to know the demands of UPSC CSE. One must not be bothered about the utility of the time spent while going through this booklet as Abraham Lincoln once rightly said, "Give me six hours to chop down a tree and I will spend the first four sharpening the axe."

Going through the syllabus is not the end. But it is, perhaps, the end of the beginning. By putting the syllabus on your fingertips, you may have just started the CSE journey. Henceforth, you should move towards making a strategy and then its execution. This is because success comes from flawless execution of the strategy.

We wish you all the best for your UPSC CSE journey.

With Best Regards,

Editor-in-Chief

Drishti Publications

Civil Services Examination

Preliminary Examination of the Civil Services Examination for recruitment to the Services and Posts mentioned below are held by the Union Public Service Commission in accordance with the Rules published by the Department of Personnel & Training. The examination is conducted for the following services.

1. Indian Administrative Service
2. Indian Foreign Service
3. Indian Police Service
4. Indian Audit and Accounts Service, Group 'A'
5. Indian Civil Accounts Service, Group 'A'
6. Indian Corporate Law Service, Group 'A'
7. Indian Defence Accounts Service, Group 'A'
8. Indian Defence Estates Service, Group 'A'
9. Indian Information Service, Group 'A'
10. Indian Postal Service, Group 'A'
11. Indian P&T Accounts and Finance Service, Group 'A'
12. Indian Railway Protection Force Service, Group 'A'
13. Indian Revenue Service (Customs & Indirect Taxes) Group 'A'
14. Indian Revenue Service (Income Tax) Group 'A'
15. Indian Trade Service, Group 'A' (Grade III)
16. Indian Railway Management Service, Group 'A'
17. Armed Forces Headquarters Civil Service, Group 'B' (Section Officer's Grade)
18. Delhi, Andaman and Nicobar Islands, Lakshadweep, Daman & Diu and Dadra & Nagar Haveli Civil Service (DANICS), Group 'B'
19. Delhi, Andaman and Nicobar Islands, Lakshadweep, Daman & Diu and Dadra & Nagar Haveli Police Service (DANIPS), Group 'B'
20. Pondicherry Civil Service (PONDICS), Group 'B'
21. Pondicherry Police Service (PONDIPS), Group 'B'

SECTION – I: PLAN OF EXAMINATION

The Civil Services Examination will consist of two successive stages:

- Civil Services (Preliminary) Examination (Objective Type) for the selection of candidates for Main Examination; and
- Civil Services (Main) Examination (Written and Interview) for the selection of candidates for the various Services and posts.

The Preliminary Examination will consist of two papers of Objective type (multiple choice questions) and carry a maximum of 400 marks in the subjects set out in sub-section (A) of Section

This examination is meant to serve as a screening test only; the marks obtained in the Preliminary Examination by the candidates who are declared qualified for admission to the Main Examination will not be counted for determining their final order of merit. The number of candidates to be admitted to the Main Examination will be about twelve to thirteen times the total approximate number of vacancies to be filled in the year through this examination. Only those candidates who are declared by the Commission to have qualified in the Preliminary Examination in the year will be eligible for admission to the Main Examination of that year provided they are otherwise eligible for admission, to the Main Examination.

Note I: The Commission will draw a list of candidates to be qualified for Civil Services (Main) Examination based on the criterion of minimum qualifying marks of 33% in General Studies Paper-II of Civil Services (Preliminary) Examination and total qualifying marks of General Studies Paper-I of Civil Services (Preliminary) Examination as may be determined by the Commission.

Note II: There will be negative marking for incorrect answers (as detailed below) for all questions except some of the questions where the negative marking will be inbuilt in the form of different marks being awarded to the most appropriate and not so appropriate answer for such questions.

- There are four alternatives for the answers to every question. For each question for which a wrong answer has been given by the candidate, one-third (0.33) of the marks assigned to that question will be deducted as penalty.
- If a candidate gives more than one answer, it will be treated as a wrong answer even if one of the given answers happen to be correct and there will be same penalty as above for that question.
- If a question is left blank i.e. no answer is given by the candidate, there will be no penalty for that question.

The Main Examination will consist of written examination and an interview test. The written examination will consist of 9 papers of conventional essay type in the subjects set out in sub-section (B) of Section II out of which two papers will be of qualifying in nature. Also see Note (ii) under Para I of Section II (B) Marks obtained for all the compulsory papers (Paper-I to Paper-VII) and Marks obtained in Interview for Personality Test will be counted for ranking.

Candidates who obtain such minimum qualifying marks in the written part of the Main Examination as may be fixed by the Commission at their discretion, shall be summoned by them for an interview for a Personality Test, vide sub-section 'C' of Section II. The number of candidates to be summoned for interview will be about twice of the number of vacancies to be filled. The interview will carry 275 marks (with no minimum qualifying marks).

Marks thus obtained by the candidates in the Main Examination (written part as well as interview) would determine their final ranking. Candidates will be allotted to the various Services keeping in view their ranks in the examination and the preferences expressed by them for the various Services and posts.

SECTION – II: SCHEME AND SUBJECTS FOR THE PRELIMINARY AND MAIN EXAMINATION

A. Preliminary Examination

The Examination shall comprise of two compulsory Papers of 200 marks each.

NOTE: Both the question papers will be of the objective type (multiple choice questions) and each will be of two hours duration.

- The General Studies Paper-II of the Civil Services (Preliminary) Examination will be a qualifying paper with minimum qualifying marks fixed at 33%.
- The question papers will be set both in Hindi and English.
- Details of the syllabi are indicated in Part A of Section III.

B. Main Examination

The written examination will consist of the following papers

Qualifying Papers:

Paper-A: (One of the Indian Language to be selected by

the candidate from the Languages included in the Eighth Schedule to the Constitution). **300 Marks**

Paper-B: English **300 Marks**

Papers to be counted for merit

Paper-I: Essay **250 Marks**

Paper-II: General Studies-I **250 Marks**

(Indian Heritage and Culture, History and Geography of the World and Society)

Paper-III: General Studies -II **250 Marks**

(Governance, Constitution, Polity, Social Justice and International relations)

Paper-IV: General Studies -III **250 Marks**

(Technology, Economic Development, Bio-diversity, Environment, Security and Disaster Management)

Paper-V: General Studies -IV **250 Marks**

(Ethics, Integrity and Aptitude)

Paper-VI: Optional Subject - Paper 1	**250 Marks**
Paper-VII: Optional Subject - Paper 2	**250 Marks**
Sub Total (Written test)	**1750 Marks**
Personality Test	**275 Marks**
Grand Total	**2025 Marks**

Candidates may choose any one of the optional subjects from amongst the list of subjects given in the table below.

NOTE:

- The papers on Indian languages and English (Paper A and paper B) will be of Matriculation or equivalent standard and will be of qualifying nature. The marks obtained in these papers will not be counted for ranking.
- Evaluation of the papers, namely, 'Essay', 'General Studies' and Optional Subject of all the candidates would be done simultaneously along with evaluation of their qualifying papers on 'Indian Languages' and 'English' but the papers on Essay, General Studies and Optional Subject of only such candidates will be taken cognizance who attain 25% marks in 'Indian Language' and 25% in English as minimum qualifying standards in these qualifying papers.
- The paper A on Indian Language will not, however, be compulsory for candidates hailing from the States of Arunachal Pradesh, Manipur, Meghalaya, Mizoram, Nagaland and Sikkim.
- The paper A on Indian Language will not, however, be compulsory for Candidates belonging to Persons with Benchmark Disabilities (only Hearing Impairment sub-category) provided that they have been granted such exemption from 2nd or 3rd language courses by the concerned education Board/University. The candidate needs to provide an undertaking/self declaration in this regard in order to claim such an exemption to the Commission.
- Marks obtained by the candidates for the Paper I-VII only will be counted for merit ranking. However, the Commission will have the discretion to fix qualifying marks in any or all of these papers.
- For the Language medium/literature of languages, the scripts to be used by the candidates will be as under:—

Language	Script
Assamese	Assamese
Bengali	Bengali
Gujarati	Gujarati
Hindi	Devanagari
Kannada	Kannada
Kashmiri	Persian
Konkani	Devanagari
Malayalam	Malayalam
Manipuri	Bengali
Marathi	Devanagari
Nepali	Devanagari
Odia	Odia
Punjabi	Gurumukhi
Sanskrit	Devanagari
Sindhi	Devanagari or Arabic
Tamil	Tamil
Telugu	Telugu
Urdu	Persian
Bodo	Devanagari
Dogri	Devanagari
Maithilli	Devanagari
Santhali	Devanagari or Olchiki

NOTE: For Santhali language, question paper will be printed in Devanagari script; but candidates will be free to answer either in Devanagari script or in Olchiki.

List of optional subjects for Main Examination	
Agriculture	Management
Animal Husbandry and Veterinary Science	Mathematics
Anthropology	Mechanical Engineering

Contd...

List of optional subjects for Main Examination	
Botany	Medical Science
Chemistry	Philosophy
Civil Engineering	Physics
Commerce and Accountancy	Political Science and International Relations
Economics	Psychology
Electrical Engineering	Public Administration
Geography	Sociology
Geology	Statistics
History	Zoology
Law	

Literature of any one of the following languages
Assamese, Bengali, Bodo, Dogri, Gujarati, Hindi, Kannada, Kashmiri, Konkani, Maithili, Malayalam, Manipuri, Marathi, Nepali, Odia, Punjabi, Sanskrit, Santhali, Sindhi, Tamil, Telugu, Urdu and English.

NOTE:

- The question papers for the examination will be of conventional (essay) type.
- Each paper will be of three hours duration.
- Candidates will have the option to answer all the question papers, except the Qualifying Language Papers, Paper-A and Paper-B, in any one of the languages included in the Eighth Schedule to the Constitution of India or in English. Notwithstanding this, the Candidate will have the choice to write the Optional Papers in English also if candidates opt to write Paper I-V except the Qualifying Language Papers, Paper-A and Paper-B, in any one of the language included in the Eighth Schedule to the Constitution of India.
- Candidates exercising the option to answer Papers in any one of the languages included in the Eight Schedule to the Constitution of India mentioned above may, if they so desire, give English version within brackets of only the description of the technical terms, if any, in addition to the version in the language opted by them. Candidates should, however, note that if they misuse the above rule, a deduction will be made on this account from the total marks otherwise accruing to them and in extreme cases; their script(s) will not be valued for being in an unauthorized medium. Candidates should note that if any irrelevant matter/

signages/marks etc. are found written in the answer script(s), which would not be related to any question/answer and/or would be having the potential to disclose the candidate's identity, the Commission will impose a penalty of deduction of marks from the total marks otherwise accruing to the candidate or will not evaluate the said script(s) on this account.

- The question papers (other than the literature of language papers) will be set in Hindi and English only.
- The details of the syllabi are set out in Part B of Section III.

It is also important to note that candidates are not permitted to use calculators for answering objective type papers (Test Booklets). They should not therefore bring the same inside the Examination Hall.

Interview Test

The candidate will be interviewed by a Board who will have before them a record of his career. He will be asked questions on matters of general interest. The object of the interview is to assess the personal suitability of the candidate for a career in public service by a Board of competent and unbiased observers. The test is intended to judge the mental caliber of a candidate. In broad terms this is really an assessment of not only his intellectual qualities but also social traits and his interest in current affairs. Some of the qualities to be judged are mental alertness, critical powers of assimilation, clear and logical exposition, balance of judgement, variety and depth of interest, ability for social cohesion and leadership, intellectual and moral integrity.

The technique of the interview is not that of a strict cross-examination but of a natural, though directed and purposive conversation which is intended to reveal the mental qualities of the candidate.

The interview test is not intended to be a test either of the specialised or general knowledge of the candidates which has been already tested through their written papers. Candidates are expected to have taken an intelligent interest not only in their special subjects of academic study but also in the events which are happening around them both within and outside their own State or Country as well as in modern currents of thought and in new discoveries which should rouse the curiosity of well educated youth.

SECTION – III: SYLLABI FOR THE EXAMINATION

NOTE: Candidates are advised to go through the Syllabus published in this Section for the Preliminary Examination and the Main Examination, as periodic revision of syllabus has been done in several subjects.

Part A – Preliminary Examination

Paper I: (200 marks) **Duration: Two hours**

- Current events of national and international importance.
- History of India and Indian National Movement.
- Indian and World Geography-Physical, Social, Economic Geography of India and the World.
- Indian Polity and Governance-Constitution, Political System, Panchayati Raj, Public Policy, Rights Issues, etc.
- Economic and Social Development-Sustainable Development, Poverty, Inclusion, Demographics, Social Sector Initiatives, etc.
- General issues on Environmental ecology, Bio-diversity and Climate Change - that do not require subject specialization.
- General Science.

Paper II: (200 marks) **Duration: Two hours**

- Comprehension;
- Interpersonal skills including communication skills;
- Logical reasoning and analytical ability;
- Decision making and problem solving;
- General mental ability;
- Basic numeracy (numbers and their relations, orders of magnitude, etc.) (Class X level), Data interpretation (charts, graphs, tables, data sufficiency etc. — Class X level);

NOTE 1: Paper-II of the Civil Services (Preliminary) Examination will be a qualifying paper with minimum qualifying marks fixed at 33%.

NOTE 2: The questions will be of multiple choice, objective type.

NOTE 3: It is mandatory for the candidate to appear in both the Papers of Civil Services (Prelim) Examination for the purpose of evaluation. Therefore a candidate will be disqualified in case he/she does not appear in both the papers of Civil Services (Prelim) Examination.

Part B – Main Examination

The main Examination is intended to assess the overall intellectual traits and depth of understanding of candidates rather than merely the range of their information and memory.

The nature and standard of questions in the General Studies papers (Paper II to Paper V) will be such that a well-educated person will be able to answer them without any specialized study. The questions will be such as to test a candidate's general awareness of a variety of subjects, which will have relevance for a career in Civil Services. The questions are likely to test the candidate's basic understanding of all relevant issues, and ability to analyze, and take a view on conflicting socio-economic goals, objectives and demands. The candidates must give relevant, meaningful and succinct answers.

The scope of the syllabus for optional subject papers (Paper VI and Paper VII) for the examination is broadly of the honours degree 1evel i.e. a level higher than the bachelors' degree and lower than the masters' degree. In the case of Engineering, Medical Science and law, the level corresponds to the bachelors' degree.

Syllabi of the papers included in the scheme of Civil Services (Main) Examination are given as follows:—

Qualifying Papers On Indian Languages And English

The aim of the paper is to test the candidates' ability to read and understand serious discursive prose, and to express his ideas clearly and correctly, in English and Indian language concerned.

The pattern of questions would be broadly as follows:

- Comprehension of given passages.
- Précis Writing.
- Usage and Vocabulary.
- Short Essays.

Indian Languages:

- comprehension of given passages.
- Précis Writing.
- Usage and Vocabulary.
- Short Essays.
- Translation from English to the Indian Language and vice-versa.

NOTE 1: The papers on Indian Languages and English will be of Matriculation or equivalent standard and will be of qualifying nature only. The marks obtained in these papers will not be counted for ranking.

NOTE 2: The candidates will have to answer the English and Indian Languages papers in English and the respective Indian language (except where translation is involved).

Paper-I

Essay: Candidates may be required to write essays on multiple topics. They will be expected to keep closely to the subject of the essay to arrange their ideas in orderly fashion, and to write concisely. Credit will be given for effective and exact expression.

Paper-II

General Studies-I: Indian Heritage and Culture, History and Geography of the World and Society.

- Indian culture will cover the salient aspects of Art Forms, literature and Architecture from ancient to modern times.
- Modern Indian history from about the middle of the eighteenth century until the present- significant events, personalities, issues.
- The Freedom Struggle — its various stages and important contributors/ contributions from different parts of the country.
- Post-independence consolidation and reorganization within the country.
- History of the world will include events from 18th century such as industrial revolution, world wars, redrawal of national boundaries, colonization, decolonization, political philosophies like communism, capitalism, socialism etc. – their forms and effect on the society.
- Salient features of Indian Society, Diversity of India.
- Role of women and women's organization, population and associated issues, poverty and developmental issues, urbanization, their problems and their remedies.
- Effects of globalization on Indian society.
- Social empowerment, communalism, regionalism & secularism.
- Salient features of world's physical geography.

- Distribution of key natural resources across the world (including South Asia and the Indian sub-continent); factors responsible for the location of primary, secondary, and tertiary sector industries in various parts of the world (including India).
- Important Geophysical phenomena such as earthquakes, Tsunami, Volcanic activity, cyclone etc., geographical features and their location-changes in critical geographical features (including water-bodies and ice-caps) and in flora and fauna and the effects of such changes.

Paper-III

General Studies- II: Governance, Constitution, Polity, Social Justice and International relations.

- Indian Constitution—historical underpinnings, evolution, features, amendments, significant provisions and basic structure.
- Functions and responsibilities of the Union and the States, issues and challenges pertaining to the federal structure, devolution of powers and finances up to local levels and challenges therein.
- Separation of powers between various organs dispute redressal mechanisms and institutions.
- Comparison of the Indian constitutional scheme with that of other countries.
- Parliament and State legislatures—structure, functioning, conduct of business, powers & privileges and issues arising out of these.
- Structure, organization and functioning of the Executive and the Judiciary—Ministries and Departments of the Government; pressure groups and formal/informal associations and their role in the Polity.
- Salient features of the Representation of People's Act.
- Appointment to various Constitutional posts, powers, functions and responsibilities of various Constitutional Bodies.
- Statutory, regulatory and various quasi-judicial bodies.
- Government policies and interventions for development in various sectors and issues arising out of their design and implementation.
- Development processes and the development industry —the role of NGOs, SHGs, various groups and associations, donors, charities, institutional and other stakeholders.

- Welfare schemes for vulnerable sections of the population by the Centre and States and the performance of these schemes; mechanisms, laws, institutions and Bodies constituted for the protection and betterment of these vulnerable sections.
- Issues relating to development and management of Social Sector/Services relating to Health, Education, Human Resources.
- Issues relating to poverty and hunger.
- Important aspects of governance, transparency and accountability, e-governance-applications, models, successes, limitations, and potential; citizens charters, transparency & accountability and institutional and other measures.
- Role of civil services in a democracy.
- India and its neighborhood- relations.
- Bilateral, regional and global groupings and agreements involving India and/or affecting India's interests.
- Effect of policies and politics of developed and developing countries on India's interests, Indian diaspora.
- Important International institutions, agencies and fora- their structure, mandate.

Paper-IV

General Studies-III: Technology, Economic Development, Bio diversity, Environment, Security and Disaster Management

- Indian Economy and issues relating to planning, mobilization, of resources, growth, development and employment.
- Inclusive growth and issues arising from it.
- Government Budgeting.
- Major crops-cropping patterns in various parts of the country, - different types of irrigation and irrigation systems storage, transport and marketing of agricultural produce and issues and related constraints; e-technology in the aid of farmers.
- Issues related to direct and indirect farm subsidies and minimum support prices; Public Distribution System- objectives, functioning, limitations, revamping; issues of buffer stocks and food security; Technology missions; economics of animal-rearing.
- Food processing and related industries in India- scope' and significance, location, upstream and downstream requirements, supply chain management.

- Land reforms in India.
- Effects of liberalization on the economy, changes in industrial policy and their effects on industrial growth.
- Infrastructure: Energy, Ports, Roads, Airports, Railways etc.
- Investment models.
- Science and Technology- developments and their applications and effects in everyday life.
- Achievements of Indians in science & technology; indigenization of technology and developing new technology.
- Awareness in the fields of IT, Space, Computers, robotics, nano-technology, bio-technology and issues relating to intellectual property rights.
- Conservation, environmental pollution and degradation, environmental impact assessment.
- Disaster and disaster management.
- Linkages between development and spread of extremism.
- Role of external state and non-state actors in creating challenges to internal security.
- Challenges to internal security through communication networks, role of media and social networking sites in internal security challenges, basics of cyber security; money-laundering and its prevention.
- Security challenges and their management in border areas - linkages of organized crime with terrorism.
- Various Security forces and agencies and their mandate.

Paper-V

General Studies- IV: Ethics, Integrity and Aptitude

This paper will include questions to test the candidates' attitude and approach to issues relating to integrity, probity in public life and his problem solving approach to various issues and conflicts faced by him in dealing with society. Questions may utilise the case study approach to determine these aspects. The following broad areas will be covered:

- Ethics and Human Interface: Essence, determinants and consequences of Ethics in-human actions; dimensions of ethics; ethics - in private and public relationships. Human Values - lessons from the lives and teachings of great leaders, reformers and administrators; role of family society and educational institutions in inculcating values.

- Attitude: content, structure, function; its influence and relation with thought and behaviour; moral and political attitudes; social influence and persuasion.
- Aptitude and foundational values for Civil Service, integrity, impartiality and non-partisanship, objectivity, dedication to public service, empathy, tolerance and compassion towards the weaker-sections.
- Emotional intelligence-concepts, and their utilities and application in administration and governance.
- Contributions of moral thinkers and philosophers from India and world.
- Public/Civil service values and Ethics in Public administration: Status and problems; ethical concerns and dilemmas in government and private institutions; laws, rules, regulations and conscience as sources of ethical guidance; accountability and ethical governance; strengthening of ethical and moral values in governance; ethical issues in international relations and funding; corporate governance.
- Probity in Governance: Concept of public service; Philosophical basis of governance and probity; Information sharing and transparency in government, Right to Information, Codes of Ethics, Codes of Conduct, Citizen's Charters, Work culture, Quality of service delivery, Utilization of public funds, challenges of corruption.
- Case Studies on above issues.

Paper-VI & Paper VII

Optional Subject Papers I & II – Candidate may choose any optional subject from amongst the List of Optional Subjects stated below.

AGRICULTURE

Paper-I

Ecology and its relevance to man, natural resources, their sustainable management and conservation. Physical and social environment as factors of crop distribution and production. Agro ecology; cropping pattern as indicators of environments. Environmental pollution and associated hazards to crops, animals and humans. Climate change—International conventions and global initiatives. Green house effect and global warming. Advance tools for ecosystem analysis—Remote Sensing (RS) and Geographic Information Systems (GIS).

Cropping patterns in different agro-climatic zones of the country. Impact of high-yielding and short-duration varieties on shifts in cropping patterns. Concepts of various cropping, and farming systems. Organic and Precision farming. Package of practices for production of important cereals, pulses, oil seeds, fibres, sugar, commercial and fodder crops.

Important features, and scope of various types of forestry plantations such as social forestry, agro-forestry, and natural forests: Propagation of forest plants. Forest products. Agro-forestry and value addition. Conservation of forest flora and fauna.

Weeds, their characteristics, dissemination and association with various crops; their multiplications; cultural, biological, and chemical control of weeds.

Soil—physical, chemical and biological properties. Processes and factors of soil formation. Soils of India. Mineral and organic constituents of soils and their role in maintaining soil productivity. Essential plant nutrients and other beneficial elements in soils and plants. Principles of soil fertility, soil testing and fertiliser recommendations, integrated nutrient management Biofertilizers. Losses of nitrogen in soil, nitrogen-use efficiency in submerged rice soils, nitrogen fixation in soils. Efficient phosphoruse and potassium use. Problem soils and their reclamation. Soil factors affecting green house gas emission.

Soil conservation, integrated watershed management. Soil erosion and its management. Dry land agriculture and its problems. Technology for stabilising agriculture production in rainfed areas.

Water-use efficiency in relation to crop production, criteria for scheduling irrigations, ways and means of reducing run-off losses of irrigation water. Rainwater harvesting. Drip and sprinkler irrigation. Drainage of water-logged soils, quality of irrigation water, effect of industrial effluents on soil and water pollution. Irrigation projects in India.

Farm management, scope, importance and characteristics, farm planning. Optimum resource use and budgeting. Economics of different types of farming systems. Marketing management strategies for development, market intelligence. Price fluctuations and their cost; role of co-operatives in agricultural economy; types and systems of farming and factors affecting them. Agricultural price policy. Crop Insurance.

Agricultural extension, its importance and role, methods of evaluation of extension programmes, socio-economic survey and status of big, small and marginal farmers and landless agricultural labourers; Training programmes for extension workers. Role of Krishi Vigyan Kendra's (KVK) in dissemination of Agricultural technologies. Non-Government Organisation (NGO) and self-help group approach for rural development.

Paper-II

Cell structure, function and cell cycle. Synthesis, structure and function of genetic material. Laws of heredity. Chromosome structure, chromosomal aberrations, linkage and cross-over, and their significance in recombination breeding. Polyploidy, euploids and aneuploids. Mutation—and their role in crop improvement. Heritability, sterility and incompatibility, classification and their application in crop improvement. Cytoplasmic inheritance, sex-linked, sex-influenced and sex-limited characters.

History of plant breeding. Modes of reproduction, selfing and crossing techniques. Origin, evolution and domestication of crop plants, center of origin, law of homologous series, crop genetic resources—conservation and utilization. Application of principles of plant breeding, improvement of crop plants. Molecular markers and their application in plant improvement. Pure-line selection, pedigree, mass and recurrent selections, combining ability, its significance in plant breeding. Heterosis and its exploitation. Somatic hybridization. Breeding for disease and pest resistance. Role of interspecific and intergeneric hybridization. Role of genetic engineering and biotechnology in crop improvement Gernetically modified crop plants.

Seed production and processing technologies. Seed certification, Seed testing and storage. DNA finger printing and seed registration. Role of public and private sectors in seed production, and marketing. Intellectual Property Rights (IPR) Issues, WTO Issues and its impact on Agriculture.

Principles of Plant Physiology with reference to plant nutrition, absorption, translocation and metabolism of nutrients. Soil-water-plant relationship.

Enzymes and plant pigments; photosynthesis—modern concepts and factors affecting the process, aerobic and anaerobic respiration; C3, C4 and CAM mechanisms. Carbohydrate, protein and fat metabolism. Growth and development; photoperiodism and vernalization. Plant growth substances and their role in crop production. Physiology of seed development and germination; dormancy. Stress physiology—draught, salt and water stress.

Major fruits, plantation crops, vegetables, spices and flower crops. Package practices of major horticultural crops. Protected cultivation and high tech horticulture. Post-harvest technology and value addition of fruits and vegetables. Landscaping and commercial floriculture. Medicinal and aromatic plants. Role of fruits and vegetables in human nutrition.

Diagnosis of pests and diseases of field crops, vegetables, orchard and plantation crops and their economic importance. Classification of pests and diseases and their management. Intergrated pest and diseases management. Storage pests and their management. Biological control of pests and diseases. Epidemiology and forecasting of major crop pests and diseases. Plant quarantine measures. Pesticides, their formulation and modes of action.

Food production and consumption trends in India. Food security and growing population—vision 2020. Reasons for grain surplus. National and International food policies. Production, procurement, distribution constraints. Availability of foodgtrains, per capita expenditure on food. Trends in poverty, Public Distribution System and Below Poverty Line population, Targeted Public Distribution System (PDS), policy implementation in context to globalization. Processing constraints. Relation of food production to National Dietary Guidelines and food consumption pattern. Food based dietary approaches to eliminate hunger. Nutrient deficiency—Micro nutrient deficiency: Protein Energy Malnutrition or Protein Calorie Malnutrition (PEM or PCM), Micro nutrient deficiency and HRD in context of work capacity of women and children. Food grain productivity and food security.

ANIMAL HUSBANDRY AND VETERINARY SCIENCE

Paper-I

1. Animal Nutrition

- Partitioning of food energy within the animal. Direct and indirect calorimetry. Carbon—nitrogen balance and comparative slaughter methods. Systems for expressing energy value of foods in ruminants, pigs and poultry. Energy requirements for maintenance, growth, pregnancy, lactation, egg, wool, and meat production.
- Latest advances in protein nutrition. Energy protein inter-relationships. Evaluation of protein quality. Use of NPN compounds in ruminant diets. Protein requirements for maintenance, growth, pregnancy, lactation, egg, wool and meat production.
- Major and trace minerals—Their sources, physiological functions and deficiency symptoms. Toxic minerals. Mineral interactions. Role of fatsoluble and water—soluble vitamins in the body, their sources and deficiency symptoms.
- Feed additives—methane inhibitors, probiotics, enzymes, antibiotics, hormones, oligosaccharides, antioxidants, emulsifiers, mould inhibitors, buffers etc. Use and abuse of growth promoters like harmones and antibiotics—latest concepts.
- Conservation of fodders. Storage of feeds and feed ingredients. Recent advances in feed technology and feed processing. Anti-nutritional and toxic factors present in livestock feeds. Feed analysis and quality control. Digestibility trials—direct, indirect and indicator methods. Predicting feed intake in grazing animals.
- Advances in ruminant nutrition. Nutrient requirements. Balanced rations. Feeding of calves, pregnant, work animals and breeding bulls. Strategies for feeding milch animals during different stages of lactation cycle. Effect of feeding on milk composition. Feeding of goats for meat and milk production. Feeding of sheep for meat and wool production.
- Swine Nutrition Nutrient requirements. Creep, starter, grower and finisher rations. Feeding of pigs for lean meat production. Low cost rations for swine.
- Poultry nutrition. Special features of poultry nutrition. Nutrient requirements for meat and egg production. Formulation of rations for different classes of layers and broilers.

2. Animal Physiology

- Physiology of blood and its circulation, respiration; excretion. Endocrine glands in health and disease.

- Blood constituents.—Properties and functions-blood cell formation—Haemoglobin synthesis and chemistry-plasma proteins production, classification and properties, coagulation of blood; Haemorrhagic disorders—anti-coagulants—blood groups—Blood volume—Plasma expanders-Buffer systems in blood. Biochemical tests and their significance in disease diagnosis.
- Circulation.—Physiology of heart, cardiac cycle, heart sounds, heart beat, electrocardiograms. Work and efficiency of heart—effect of ions on heart function-metabolism of cardiac muscle, nervous and chemical regulation of heart, effect of temperature and stress on heart, blood pressuer and hypertension, osmotic regulation, arterial pulse, vasomotor regulation of circulation, shock. Coronary and pulmonary circulation, Blood-Brain barrier Cerebrospinal fluid-circulation in birds.
- Respiration.—Mechanism of respiration, Transport and exchange of gases-neural control of respiration-Chemo-receptors-hypoxia-respiration in birds.
- Excretion.—Structure and function of kidney-formation of urine-methods of studying renal function-renal regulation of acid-base balance: physiological constituents of urine-renal failure-passive venous congestion-Urinary secretion in chicken-Sweat glands and their function. Bio-chemical test for urinary dysfunction.
- Endocrine glands.—Functional disorders—their symptoms and diagnosis. Synthesis of hormones, mechanism and control of secretion—hormonal receptors-classification and function.
- Growth and Animal Production.—Prenatal and postnatal growth, maturation, growth curves, measures of growth, factors affecting growth, conformation, body composition, meat quality.
- Physiology of Milk Production, Reproduction and Digestion.—Current status of hormonal control of mammary development, milk secretion and milk ejection. Male and Female reproductive organs, their components and functions. Digestive organs and their functions.
- Environmental Physiology.—Physiological relations and their regulation; mechanisms of adaptation, environmental factors and regulatory mechanisms involved in animal behaviour, climatology—various parameters and their importance. Animal ecology. Physiology of behaviour. Effect of stress on health and production.

3. Animal Reproduction

Semen quality—Preservation and Artificial Insemination—Components of semen, composition of spermatozoa, chemical and physical properties of ejaculated semen, factors affecting semen in vivo and in vitro. Factors affecting semen production and quality, preservation, composition of diluents, sperm concentration, transport of diluted semen. Deep freezing techniques in cows, sheep, goats, swine and poultry. Detection of oestrus and time of insemination for better conception. Anoestrus and repeat breeding.

4. Livestock Production and Management

- Commercial Dairy Farming.—Comparison of dairy farming in India with advanced countries. Dairying under mixed farming and as specialized farming, economic dairy farming. Starting of a dairy farm, Capital and land requirement, organization of the dairy farm. Opportunities in dairy farming, factors determining the efficiency of dairy animal. Heard recording, budgeting cost of milk production, pricing policy; Personnel Management. Developing Practical and Economic rations for dairy cattle; supply of greens throughout the year, feed and fodder requirements of Dairy Farm. Feeding regimes for young stock and bulls, heifers and breeding animals; new trends in feeding young and adult stock; Feeding records.
- Commercial meat, egg and wool production.—Development of practical and economic rations for sheep, goats, pigs, rabbits and poultry. Supply of greens, fodder, feeding regimes for young and mature stock. New trends in enhancing production and management. Capital and land requirements and socio-economic concept.
- Feeding and management of animals under drought, flood and other natural calamities.

5. Genetics and Animal Breeding

- History of animal genetics. Mitosis and Meiosis: Mendelian inheritance; deviations to Mendelian genetics; Expression of genes; Linkage and crossing over; Sex determination, sex influenced and sex limited characters; Blood groups and polymorphism; Chromosome aberrations; Cytoplasmic inheritance, Gene and its structure; DNA as a genetic material; Genetic code and protein synthesis; Recombinant DNA technology. Mutations, types of mutations, methods for detecting mutations and mutation rate, Transgenesis.
- Population Genetics applied to Animal Breeding—Quantitative Vs. Qualitative traits; Hardy Weinberg Law; Population Vs. Individual; Gene and genotypic frequency; Forces changing gene frequency; Random drift and small populations; Theory of path coefficient; Inbreeding, methods of estimating inbreeding coefficient, systems of inbreeding; Effective population size; Breeding value,

estimation of breeding value, dominance and epistatic deviation; Partitioning of variation; Genotype X environment correlation and genotype X environment interaction; role of multiple measurements; Resemblance between relatives.

- Breeding Systems.—Breeds of livestsock and Poultry. Heritability, repeatability and genetic and phenotypic correlations, their methods of estimation and precision of estimates; Aids to selection and their relative merits; Individual, pedigree, family and within family selection; Pregnency testing; Methods of selection; Construction of selection indices and their uses; Comparative evaluation of genetic gains through various selection methods; Indirect selection and correlated response; Inbreeding, out breeding, upgrading, cross-breeding and synthesis of breeds; Crossing of inbred lines for commercial production; Selection for general and specific combining ability; Breeding for threshold characters. Sire index.

6. Extension

Basic philosophy, objectives, concept and principles of extension. Different Methods adopted to educate farmers under rural conditions. Generation of technology, its transfer and feedback. Problems and constraints in transfer of technology. Animal husbandry programmes for rural development.

Paper-II

1. Anatomy, Pharmacology and Hygiene

- **Histology and Histological Techniques:** Paraffin embedding technique of tissue processing and H.E. staining—Freezing microtomy—Microscopy Bright field microscope and electron microscope. Cytology-structure of cell organells and inclusions; cell division-cell types—Tissues and their classification-embryonic and adult tissues—Comparative histology of organs—Vascular, Nervous, digestive, respiratory, musculo-skeletal and urogenital systems—Endocrine glands—Integuments—sense organs.
- **Embryology.**—Embryology of vertebrates with special reference to aves and domestic mammals gametogenesis-fertilization-germ layers-foetal membranes and placentation-types of placenta in domestic mammals-Teratology-twins and twinning-organogenesis-germ layer derivatives-endodermal, mesodermal and ectodermal derivatives.
- **Bovine Anatomy.**—Regional Anatomy: Paranasal sinuses of OX— surface anatomy of salivary glands. Regional anatomy of infraorbital, maxillary, mandibuloalveolar, mental and cornnal nerve block. Regional anatomy of paravertebral

nerves, pudental nerve, median, ulnar and radial nervestibial, fibular and digital nerves—Cranial nerves-structures involved in epidural anaesthesia-superficial lymph nodes-surface anatomy of visceral organs of thoracic, abdominal and pelvic cavities-comparative-features of locomotor apparatus and their application in the biomechanics of mammalian body.

- **Anatomy of Fowl.**—Musculo-skeletal system-functional anatomy in relation to respiration and flying, digestion and egg production.
- **Pharmacology and therapeutics drugs.**—Cellular level of pharmacodynamics and pharmacokinetics. Drugs acting on fluids and electrolyte balance. Drugs acting on Autonomic nervous system. Modern concepts of anaesthesia and dissociative anaesthetics. Autocoids. Antimicrobials and principles of chemotherapy in microbial infections. Use of hormones in therapeutics—chemotherapy of parasitic infections. Drug and economic concerns in the Edible tissues of animals—chemotherapy of Neoplastic diseases. Toxicity due to "insecticides, plants, metals, non-metals, zootoxins and mycotoxins".
- **Veterinary Hygiene with reference to water, air and habitation.**—Assessment of pollution of water, air and soil—Importance of climate in animal health—effect of environment on animal function and performance relationship between industrialisation and animal agriculture—animal housing requirements for specific categories of domestic animals viz. pregnant cows and sows, milking cows, broiler birds—stress, strain and productivity in relation to animal habitation.

2. Animal Diseases

- Etiology, epidemiology pathogenesis, symptoms, post-moretem lesions, diagnosis, and control of infectious diseases of cattle, sheep and goat, horses, pigs and poultry.
- Etiology, epidemiology, symptoms, diagnosis, treatment of production diseases of cattle, horse, pig and poultry.
- Deficiency diseases of domestic animals and birds.
- Diagnosis and treatment of non-specific conditions like impaction, Bloat, Diarrhoea, Indigestion, dehydration, stroke, poisioning.
- Diagnosis and treatment of neurological disorders.
- **Principles and methods of immunisation of animals against specific diseases—hard immunity**—disease free zones—'zero' disease concept—chemoprophylaxis.
- **Anaesthesia.**—local, regional and general-prenesthetic medication. Symptoms and surgical interference in fractures and dislocation. Hernia, choking abomassal displacement—Caesarian operations. Rumenotomy—Castrations.

- **Disease investigation techniques.**— Materials for laboratory investigation — Establishment. Animal Health Centres—Disease free zone.

3. Veterinary Public Health

- **Zoonoses**—Classification, definition, role of animals and birds in prevalence and transmission of zoonotic diseases—occupational zoonotic diseases.
- **Epidemiology**—Principle, definition of epidemiological terms, application of epidemiological measures in the study of diseases and disease control. Epidemiological features of air, water and food borne infections. OIE regulation, WTO, sanitary and phytosanitary measures.
- **Veterinary Jurisprudence**—Rules and Regulations for improvement of animal quality and prevention of animal diseases—State and Central Rules for prevention of animal and animal product borne diseases—S.P. C.A.—Veterolegal cases—Certificates—Materials and Methods of collection of samples for veterolegal investigation.

4. Milk and Milk Products Technology

- **Market Milk:** Quality, testing and grading of raw milk. Processing, packaging, storing, distribution, marketing defects and their control. Preparation of the following milks: Pasteurized, standardized, toned, double toned, sterilized, homogenized, reconstituted, recombined and flavoured milks. Preparation of cultured milks, cultures and their management, yoghurt, Dahi, Lassi and Srikhand. Preparation of flavoured and sterilized milks. Legal standards. Sanitation requirement for clean and safe milk and for the milk plant equipment.
- **Milk Products Technology:** Selection of raw materials, processing, storing, distributing and marketing milk products such as Cream, Butter, Ghee, Khoa, Channa, Cheese, condensed, evaporated, dried milk and baby food, Ice cream and Kulfi; by-products, whey products, butter milk, lactose and casein. Testing, grading, judging milk products—BIS and Agmark specifications, legal standards, quality control nutritive properties. Packaging processing and operational control. Costing of dairy products.

5. Meat Hygiene and Technology

- **Meat Hygiene**
    - Ante mortem care and management of food animals, stunning, slaughter and dressing operations; abattoir requirements and designs; Meat inspection procedures and judgement of carcass meat cuts—grading of carcass meat cuts—duties and functions of Veterinarians in wholesome meat production.

- **Hygienic methods of handling production of meat**—Spoilage of meat and control measures—Post- slaughter physicochemical changes in meat and factors that influence them—Quality improvement methods—Adulteration of meat and detection—Regulatory provisions in Meat trade and Industry.

- **Meat Technology**
  - **5.2.1 Physical and chemical characteristics of meat**—Meat emulsions—Methods of preservation of meat—Curing, canning, irradiation, packaging of meat and meat products, processing and formulations.
- **By-products**—Slaughter house by-products and their utilisation—Edible and inedible by products—Social and economic implications of proper utilisation of slaughter house by-products—Organ products for food and pharmaceuticals.
- **Poultry Products Technology**—Chemical composition and nutritive value of poultry meat, pre- slaughter care and management. Slaughtering techniques, inspection, preservation of poultry meat and products. Legal and BIS standards.
- Structure composition and nutritive value of eggs Microbial spoilage. Preservation and maintenance. Marketing of poultry meat, eggs and products.
- **Rabbit/Fur Animal farming**—Rabbit meat production. Disposal and utilization of fur and wool and recycling of waste by products. Grading of wool.

ANTHROPOLOGY

Paper-I

- Meaning, Scope and development of Anthropology.
- Relationships with other disciplines: Social Sciences, behavioural Sciences, Life Sciences, Medical Sciences, Earth Sciences and Humanities.
- Main branches of Anthropology, their scope and relevance:
  - Social-cultural Anthropology.
  - Biological Anthropology.
  - Archaeological Anthropology.
  - Linguistic Anthropology.
- Human Evolution and emergence of Man:
  - Biological and Cultural factors in human evolution.
  - Theories of Organic Evolution (Pre-Darwinian, Darwinian and Post-Darwinian).
  - Synthetic theory of evolution; Brief outline of terms and concepts of evolutionary biology (Doll's rule, Cope's rule, Gause's rule, parallelism, convergence, adaptive radiation, and mosaic evolution).
- Characteristics of Primates; Evolutionary Trend and Primate Taxonomy; Primate Adaptations; (Arboreal and Terrestrial) Primate Taxonomy; Primate Behaviour; Tertiary and Quaternary fossil primates; Living Major Primates; Comparative Anatomy of Man and Apes; Skeletal changes due to erect posture and its implications.
- Phylogenetic status, characteristics and geographical distribution of the following:
  - Plio-preleistocene hominids inSouth and East Africa—Australopithecines.
  - *Homo erectus: Africa (Paranthropus)*, Europe (Homo erectus (heidelbergensis), Asia
  - (Homo erectus javanicus, Homo erectus pekinensis.
  - Neanderthal man—La-chapelle-aûx-saints (Classical type), Mt. Carmel (Progressive type).
  - Rhodesian man.
  - *Homo saoiens*—Cromagnon, Grimaldi and Chancelede.

The biological basis of Life: The Cell, DNA structure and replication, Protein Synthesis, Gene, Mutation, Chromosomes, and Cell Division.

- Principles of Prehistoric Archaeology. Chronology: Relative and Absolute Dating methods.
- Cultural Evolution—Broad Outlines of Prehistoric cultures:
  - Paleolithic
  - Mesolithic
  - Neolithic
  - Chalcolithic
  - Copper-Bronze Age
  - Iron Age
- **The Nature of Culture:** The concept and Characteristics of culture and civilization; Ethnocentrism vis-a-vis cultural Relativism.
- **The Nature of Society:** Concept of Society; Society and Culture; Social Institution; Social groups; and Social stratification.
- **Marriage:** Definition and universality; Laws of marriage (endogamy, exogamy, hypergamy, hypogamy, incest taboo); Type of marriage (monogamy, polygamy, polyandry, group marriage). Functions of marriage; Marriage regulations (preferential, prescriptive and proscriptive); Marriage payments (bride wealth and dowry).
- **Family:** Definition and universality; Family, household and domestic groups; functions of family; Types of family (from the perspectives of structure, blood relation, marriage, residence and succession); Impact of urbanization, industrialization and feminist movements on family.
- **Kinship:** Consanguinity and Affinity; Principles and types of descent (Unilineal, Double, Bilateral Ambilineal); Forms of descent groups (lineage, clan, phratry, moiety and kindred); Kinship terminology (descriptive and classificatory); Descent, Filiation and Complimentary Filiation;Decent and Alliance.
- **Economic Organization:** Meaning, scope and relevance of economic anthropology; Formalist and Substantivist debate; Principles governing production, distribution and exchange (reciprocity, redistribution and market), in communities, subsisting on hunting and gathering, fishing, swiddening, pastoralism, horticulture, and agriculture; globalization and indigenous economic systems.
- **Political Organization and Social Control:** Band, tribe, chiefdom, kingdom and state; concepts of power, authority and legitimacy; social control, law and justice in simple Societies.
- **Religion:** Anthropological approaches to the study of religion (evolutionary, psychological and functional); monotheism and polytheism; sacred and profane;

myths and rituals; forms of religion in tribal and peasant Societies (animism, animatism, fetishism, naturism and totemism); religion, magic and science distinguished; magico-religious functionaries (priest, shaman, medicine man, sorcerer and witch).

- **Anthropological theories:**
  - Classical evolutionism (Tylor, Morgan and Frazer)
  - Historical particularism (Boas) Diffusionism (British, German and American)
  - Functionalism (Malinowski); Structural—Functionlism (Radcliffe-Brown)
  - Structuralism (L'evi-Strauss and E. Leach)
  - Culture and personality (Benedict, Mead, Linton, Kardiner and Cora-du Bois)
  - Neo—evolutionism (Childe, White, Steward, Sahlins and Service)
  - Cultural materialism (Harris)
  - Symbolic and interpretive theories (Turner, Schneider and Geertz)
  - Cognitive theories (Tyler, Conklin)
  - Post-modernism in anthropology.
- **Culture, Language and Communication:**
  - Nature, origin and characteristics of language; verbal and non-verbal communication; social contex of language use.
- **Research methods in Anthropology:**
  - Fieldwork tradition in anthropology
  - Distinction between technique, method and methodology
  - Tools of data collection: observation, interview, schedules, questionnaire, case study, genealogy, life-history, oral history, secondary sources of information, participatory methods.
  - Analysis, interpretation and presentation of data.
- **Human Genetics:** Methods and Application: Methods for study of genetic principles in man-family study (pedigree analysis, twin study, foster child, co-twin method, cytogenetic method, chromosomal and karyo-type analysis), biochemical methods, immunological methods, D.N.A. technology and recombinant technologies.
- Mendelian genetics in man-family study, single factor, multifactor, lethal, sub-lethal and polygenic inheritance in man.
- Concept of genetic polymorphism and selection, Mendelian population, Hardy-Weinberg law; causes and changes which bring down frequency-mutation,

isolation, migration, selection, inbreeding and genetic drift. Consanguineous and non-consanguineous mating, genetic load, genetic effect of consanguineous and cousin marriages.

- Chromosomes and chromosomal aberrations in man, methodology.
  - Numerical and structural aberrations (disorders).
  - Sex chromosomal aberration- Klinefelter (XXY), Turner (XO), Super female (XXX), intersex and other syndromic disorders.
  - Autosomal aberrations- Down syndrome, Patau, Edward and Cri-du-chat syndromes.
  - Genetic imprints in human disease, genetic screening, genetic counseling, human DNA profiling, gene mapping and genome study.
- Race and racism, biological basis of morphological variation of non-metric and characters. Racial criteria, racial traits in relation to heredity and environment; biological basis of racial classification, racial differentiation and race crossing in man.
- **Age, sex and population variation as genetic marker:** ABO, Rh blood groups, HLA Hp, transferring, Gm, blood enzymes. Physiological characteristics-Hb level, body fat, pulse rate, respiratory functions and sensory perceptions in different cultural and socio-ecomomic groups.
- **Concepts and methods of Ecological Anthropology:** Bio-cultural Adaptations—Genetic and Non-genetic factors. Man's physiological responses to environmental stresses: hot desert, cold, high altitude climate.
- **Epidemiological Anthropology:** Health and disease. Infectious and non-infectious diseases, Nutritional deficiency related diseases.
- **Concept of human growth and Development:** Stages of growth—pre-natal, natal, infant, childhood, adolescence, maturity, senescence.
  - Factors affecting growth and development genetic, environmental, biochemical, nutritional, cultural and socio-economic.
  - Ageing and senescence. Theories and observations
  - Biological and chronological longevity. Human physique and somatotypes. Methodologies for growth studies.
- Relevance of menarche, menopause and other bioevents to fertility. Fertility patterns and differentials.
- Demographic theories-biological, social and cultural.
- Biological and socio-ecological factors influencing fecundity, fertility, natality and mortality.

- **Applications of Anthropology:** Anthropology of sports, Nutritional anthropology, Anthroplogy in designing of defence and other equipments, Forensic Anthroplogy, Methods and principles of personal identification and reconstruction, Applied human genetics—Paternity diagnosis, genetic counselling and eugenics, DNA technology in diseases and medicine, serogenetics and cytogenetics in reproductive biology.

Paper-II

- **Evolution of the Indian Culture and Civilization:** Prehistoric (Palaeolithic, Mesolithic, Neolithic and Neolithic-Chalcolithic), Protohistoric (Indus Civilization). Pre-Harappan, Harappan and post-Harappan cultures. Contributions of the tribal cultures to Indian civilization.
  - **Palaeo:** Anthropological evidences from India with special reference to Siwaliks and Narmada basin (*Ramapithecus, Sivapithecus and Narmada Man*).
  - **Ethno-archaeology in India:** The concept of ethno-archaeology; Survivals and Parallels among the hunting, foraging, fishing, pastoral and peasant communities including arts and crafts producing communities.
- **Demographic profile of India:** Ethnic and linguistic elements in the Indian population and their distribution. Indian population — factors influencing its structure and growth.
- The structure and nature of traditional Indian social system — Varnashram, Purushartha, Karma, Rina and Rebirth.
  - **Caste system in India:** Structure and characteristics Varna and caste, Theories of origin of caste system, Dominant caste, Caste mobility, Future of caste system, Jajmani system. Tribe-case continuum.
  - Sacred Complex and Nature-Man-Spirit Complex.
  - Impact of Buddhism, Jainism, Islam and Christianity of Indian society.
- Emergence, growth and development in India — Contributions of the 18th, 19th and early 20th Century scholar-administrators. Contributions of Indian anthropologists to tribal and caste studies.
- **Indian Village:** Significane of village study in India; Indian village as a social system; Traditional and changing patterns of settlement and inter-caste relations; Agrarian relations in Indian villages; Impact of globalization on Indian villages.
  - Linguistic and religious minorities and their social, political and economic status.

- Indigenous and exogenous processes of socio-cultural change in Indian society: Sanskritization, Westernization, Modernization; Inter-play of little and great traditions; Panchayati Raj and social change; Media and Social change.

- **Tribal situation in India:** Bio-genetic variability, linguistic and socio-economic characteristics of the tribal populations and their distribution.
  - **Problems of the tribal Communities:** Land alienation, poverty, indebtedness, low literacy, poor educational facilities, unemployment, under- employment, health and nutrition.
  - Developmental projects and their impact on tribal displacement and problems of rehabilitation. Development of forest policy and tribals. Impact of urbanisation and industrialization on tribal populations.
- Problems of exploitation and deprivation of Scheduled Castes, Scheduled Tribes and Other Backward Classes. Constitutional safeguards for Scheduled Tribes and Scheduled Castes.
  - Social change and contemporary tribal societies: Impact of modern democratic institutions, development programmes and welfare measures on tribals and weaker sections.
  - The concept of ethnicity; Ethnic conflicts and political developments; Unrest among tribal communities; Regionalism and demand for autonomy; Pseudo-tribalism. Social change among the tribes during colonial and post-Independent India.
- Impact of Hinduism, Buddhism, Christianity, Islam and other religions on tribal societies.
  - Tribe and nation state — a comparative study of tribal communities in India and other countries.
- History of administration of tribal areas, tribal policies, plans, programmes of tribal development and their implementation. The concept of PTGs (Primitive Tribal Groups), their distribution, special programmes for their development. Role of N.G.O.s in tribal development.
  - Role of anthropology in tribal and rural development.
  - Contributions of anthropology to the understanding of regionalism, communalism and ethnic and political movements.

BOTANY

Paper-I

1. Microbiology and Plant Pathology

- Structure and reproduction/multiplication of viruses,viroids, bacteria, fungi and mycoplasma; Applications of microbiology in agriculture, industry, medicine and in control of soil and water pollution; Prion and Prion hypothesis.
- Important crop diseases caused by viruses, bacteria, mycoplasma, fungi and nematodes; Modes of infection and dissemination; Molecular basis of infection and disease resistance/defence; Physiology of parasitism and control measures. Fungal toxins. Modelling and disease forecasting; Plant quarantine.

2. Cryptogams

Algae, fungi, lichens, bryophytes, pteridophytes-structure and reproduction from evolutionary viewpoint; Distribution of Cryptogams in India and their ecological and economic importance.

3. Phanerogams

- Gymnosperms: Concept of Progymnosperms. Classification and distribution of gymnosperms. Salient features of Cycadales, Ginkgoales, Coniferales and Gnetales, their structure and reproduction. General account of Cycadofilicales, Bennettitales and Cordiaitailes; Geological time scale; Type of fossils and their study techniques.
- Angiosperms: Systematics, anatomy, embryology, palynology and phylogency.
- Taxonomic hierarchy; International Code of Botanical Nomenclature; Numerical taxomomy and chemotaxomomy; Evidence from anatomy, embryology and palynology.
- Origin and evolution of angiosperms; Comparative account of various systems of classification of angiosperms; Study of angiospermic families— Mangnoliaceae, Ranunculaceae, Brassicaceae, Rosaceae, Fabaceae, Euphorbiaceae, Malvaceae, Dipterocarpaceae, Apiaceae, Asclepiadaceae, Verbenaceae, Solanaceae, Rubiaceae, Cucurbitaceae, Asteraceae, Poaceae, Arecaceae, Liliaceae, Musaceae and Orchidaceae.
- Stomata and their types; Glandular and non-glandular trichomes; Unusual secondary growth; Anatomy of C3 and C4 plants; Xylem and phloem differentiation; Wood anatomy.
- Development of male and female gametophytes, pollination, fertilization; Endosperm—its development and function. Patterns of embryo development;

Polyembroyony, apomixes; Applications of palynology; Experimental embryology including pollen storage and test-tube fertilization.

4. Plant Resource Development

Domestication and introduction of plants; Origin of cultivated plants, Vavilov's centres of origin. Plants as sources for food, fodder, fibres, spices, beverages, edible oils, drugs, narcotics, insecticides, timber, gums, resins and dyes; latex, cellulose, starch and its products; Perfumery; Importance of Ethnobotany in Indian context; Energy plantations; Botanical Gardens and Herbaria.

5. Morphogenesis

Totipotency, polarity, symmetry and differentiation; Cell, tissue, organ and protoplast culture. Somatic hybrids and Cybrids; Micropropagation; Somaclonal variation and its applications; Pollen haploids, embryo rescue methods and their applications.

Paper-II

1. Cell Biology

Techniques of cell biology. Prokaryotic and eukaryotic cells—structural and ultrastructural details; Structure and function of extracellular matrix (cell wall) and membranes-cell adhesion, membrane transport and vesicular transport; Structure and function of cell organelles (chloroplasts, mitochondria, ER, dictyosomes ribosomes, endosomes,lysosomes, peroxisomes; Cytoskelaton and microtubules; Nucleus, nucleolus, nuclear pore complex; Chromatin and nucleosome; Cell signalling and cell receptors; Signal transduction Mitosis and meiosis; molecular basis of cell cycle. Numerical and structural variations in chromosomes and their significance; Chromatin organization and packaging of genome; Polytene chromosomes; B-chromosomes—structure, behaviour and significance.

2. Genetics, Molecular Biology and Evolution

- Development of genetics, and gene versus allele concepts (Pseudoalleles); Quantitative genetics and multiple factors; Incomplete dominance, polygenic inheritance, multiple alleles; Linkage and crossing over of gene mapping including molecular maps (idea of mapping, function); Sex chromosomes and sex-linked inheritance; sex determination and molecular basis of sex differentiation; Mutations (biochemical and molecular basis); Cytoplasmic inheritance and cytoplasmic genes (including genetics of male sterility).
- Structure and synthesis of nucleic acids and proteins; Genetic code and regulation of gene expression; Gene silencing; Multigene families; Organic evolution-evidences, mechanism and theories. Role of RNA in origin and evolution.

3. Plant Breeding, Biotechnology and Biostatistics:

Methods of plant breeding—introduction, selection and hybridization (pedigree, backcross, mass selection, bulk method); Mutation, polyploidy, male sterility and heterosis breeding. Use of apomixes in plant breeding; DNA sequencing; Genetic engineering—methods of transfer of genes; Transgenic crops and biosafety aspects; Development and use of molecular markers in plant breeding; Tools and techniques—probe, southern blotting, DNA fingerprinting, PCR and FISH. Standard deviation and coefficient of variation (CV). Tests of significance (Z-test, t-test and chi-square tests). Probability and distributions (normal, binomial and Poisson). Correlation and regression.

4. Physiology and Biochemistry

Water relations, mineral nutrition and ion transport, mineral deficiencies. Photosynthesis—photochemical reactions, photophosphorylation and carbon fixation pathways; C3, C4 and CAM pathways; Mechanism of pholem transport, Respiration (anerobic and aerobic, including fermentation)—electron transport chain and oxidative phosphorylation; Photorespiration; Chemiosmotic theory and ATP synthesis; Lipid metabolism; Nitrogen fixation and nitrogen metabolism. Enzymes, coenzymes; Energy transfer and energy conservation. Importance of secondary metabolites. Pigments as photoreceptors (plastidial pigments and phytochrome). Plant movements; Photoperiodism and flowering, vernalization, senescence; Growth substances—their chemical nature, role and applications in agri-horticulture; growth indices, growth movements. Stress physiology (heat, water, salinity, metal); Fruit and seed physiology. Dormancy, storage and germination of seed. Fruit ripening—its molecular basis and manipulation.

5. Ecology and Plant Geography

- Concept of ecosystem; Ecological factors. Concepts and dynamics of community; Plant succession. Concepts of biosphere; Ecosystems; Conservation; Pollution and its control (including phytoreme-diation); Plant indicators; Environment (Protection) Act.
- Forest types of India—'Ecological and ecomomic importance of forests, afforestation, deforestation and social forestry; Endangered plants, endemism IUCN categories, Red Data Books; Biodiversity and its conservation; Protected Area Network; Convention of Biological Diversity, Farmers' Rights; and Intellectual Property Rights; Concept of Sustainable Development; Biogeochemical cycles. Global warming and climatic change; Invasive species; Environmetal Impact Assessment; Phytogeographical regions of India.

CHEMISTRY

Paper-I

1. Atomic Structure

Heisenberg's uncertainty principle Schrodinger wave equation (time independent); Interpretation of wave function, particle in one- dimensional box, quantum numbers, hydrogen atom wave functions; Shapes of s, p and d orbitals.

2. Chemical bonding

- Ionic bond, characteristics of ionic compounds, lattice energy, Born-Haber cycle; covalent bond and its general characteristics, polarities of bonds in molecules and their dipole moments; Valence bond theory, concept of resonance and resonance energy; Molecular orbital theory (LCAO method); bonding H2 +, H2 He2 + to Ne2, NO, CO, HF, CN–,
- Comparison of valence bond and molecular orbital theories, bond order, bond strength and bond length.

3. Solid State

Crystal systems; Designation of crystal faces, lattice structures and unit cell; Bragg's law; X-ray diffraction by crystals; Close packing, radius ratio rules, calculation of some limiting radius ratio values; Structures of NaCl, ZnS, CsCl, CaF2; Stoichiometric and nonstoichiometric defects, impurity defects, semi-conductors.

4. The Gaseous State and Transport Phenomenon

Equation of state for real gases, intermolecular interactions, and critical phenomena and liquefaction of gases; Maxwell's distribution of speeds, intermolecular collisions, collisions on the wall and effusion; Thermal conductivity and viscosity of ideal gases.

5. Liquid State

Kelvin equation; Surface tension and surface enercy, wetting and contact angle, interfacial tension and capillary action.

6. Thermodynamics

Work, heat and internal energy; first law of thermodynamics. Second law of thermodynamics; entropy as a state function, entropy changes in various processes, entropy-reversibility and irreversibility, Free energy functions; Thermodynamic equation of state; Maxwell relations; Temperature, volume and pressure dependence of U, H, A, G, Cp and Cv, α and β; J-T effect and inversion temperature; criteria for equilibrium, relation between equilibrium constant and thermodynamic quantities; Nernst heat theorem, introductory idea of third law of thermodynamics.

7. Phase Equilibria and Solutions

Clausius-Clapeyron equation; phase diagram for a pure substance; phase equilibria in binary systems, partially miscible liquids—upper and lower critical solution temperatures; partial molar quantities, their significance and determination; excess thermodynamic functions and their determination.

8. Electrochemistry

- Debye-Huckel theory of strong electrolytes and Debye-Huckel limiting Law for various equilibrium and transport properties.
- Galvanic cells, concentration cells; electrochemical series, measurement of e.m.f. of cells and its applications fuel cells and batteries.
- Processes at electrodes; double layer at the interface; rate of charge transfer, current density; overpotential; electroanalytical techniques: amperometry, ion selective electrodes and their use.

9. Chemical Kinetics

Differential and integral rate equations for zeroth, first, second and fractional order reactions; Rate equations involving reverse, parallel, consecutive and chain reactions; Branching chain and explosions; effect of temperature and pressure on rate constant. Study of fast reactions by stop-flow and relaxation methods. Collisions and transition state theories.

10. Photochemistry

Absorption of light; decay of excited state by different routes; photochemical reactions between hydrogen and halogens and their quantum yields.

11. Surface Phenomena and Catalysis

Adsorption from gases and solutions on solid adsorbents; Langmuir and B.E.T. adsorption isotherms; determination of surface area, characteristics and mechanism of reaction on heterogeneous catalysts.

12. Bio-inorganic Chemistry

Metal ions in biological systems and their role in ion-transport across the membranes (molecular mechanism), oxygen-uptake proteins, cytochromes and ferrodoxins.

13. Coordination Chemistry

- Bonding in transition of metal complexes. Valence bond theory, crystal field theory and its modifications; applications of theories in the explanation of magnetism and elctronic spectra of metal complexes.
- Isomerism in coordination compounds; IUPAC nomenclature of coordination compounds; stereochemistry of complexes with 4 and 6 coordination numbers; chelate effect and polynuclear complexes; trans effect and its theories; kinetics of substitution reactions in square-planar complexes; thermodynamic and kinetic stability of complexes.
- EAN rule, Synthesis structure and reactivity of metal carbonyls; carboxylate anions, carbonyl hydrides and metal nitrosyl compounds.
- Complexes with aromatic systems, synthesis, structure and bonding in metal olefin complexes, alkyne complexes and cyclopen tadieny complexes; coordinative unsaturation, oxidative addition reactions, insertion reactions, fluxional molecules and their characterization; Compounds with metal—metal bonds and metal atom clusters.

14. Main Group Chemistry

Boranes, borazines, phosphazenes and cyclic phosphazene, silicates and silicones, Interhalogen compounds; Sulphur—nitrogen compounds, noble gas compounds.

15. General Chemistry of 'f' Block Element:

Lanthanides and actinides: separation, oxidation states, magnetic and spectral properties; lanthanide contraction.

Paper-II

1. Delocalised Covalent Bonding

Aromaticity, anti-aromaticity; annulenes, azulenes, tropolones, fulvenes, sydnones.

2. Reaction mechanisms

- General methods (both kinetic and non-kinetic) of study of mechanisms or organic reactions: isotopies, mathod cross-over experiment, intermediate trapping, stereochemistry; energy of activation; thermodynamic control and kinetic control of reactions.
- **Reactive intermediates:** Generation, geometry, stability and reactions of carboniumions and carbanions, free radicals, carbenes, benzynes and nitrenes.
- **Substitution reactions:—** SN1, SN2, and SNi, mechanisms; neighbouring group
- participation; electrophilic and nucleophilic reactions of aromatic compounds including heterocyclic compounds—pyrrole, furan, thiophene and indole.
- **Elimination reactions:—**E1, E2 and E1cb mechanisms; orientation in E2 reactions—Saytzeff and Hoffmann; pyrolytic *syn* elimination—acetate pyrolysis, Chugaev and Cope eliminations.
- **Addition reactions:—**Electrophilic addition to C=C and C=C; nucleophilic addition to C=O, C=N, conjugated olefins and carbonyls.
- **Reactions and Rearrangements:**
  - Pinacol-pinacolone, Hoffmann, Beckmann, Baeyer-Villiger, Favorskii, Fries, Claisen, Cope, Stevens and Wagner—Meerwein rearrangements.
  - Aldol condensation, Claisen condensation, Dieckmann, Perkin, Knoevenagel, Witting, Clemmensen, Wolff-Kishner, Cannizzaro and von Richter reactions; Stobbe, benzoin and acyloin condensations; Fischer indole synthesis, Skraup synthesis, Bischler-Napieralski, Sandmeyer, Reimer-Tiemann and Reformatsky reactions.

3. Pericyclic reactions

Classification and examples; Woodward-Hoffmann rules—electrocyclic reactions, cycloaddition reactions [2+2 and 4+2] and sigmatropic shifts [1, 3; 3, 3 and 1, 5], FMO approach.

4. Preparation and Properties of Polymers

- Organic polymerspolyethylene, polystyrene, polyvinyl chloride, teflon, nylon, terylene, synthetic and natural rubber.
- Biopolymers: Structure of proteins, DNA and RNA.

5. Synthetic Uses of Reagents

OsO_4, HIO_4, CrO_3, $Pb(OAc)_4$, SeO_2, NBS, B_2H_6, Na-Liquid NH_3, LiAlH4, $NaBH_4$, n-BuLi, MCPBA.

6. Photochemistry

Photochemical reactions of simple organic compounds, excited and ground states, singlet and triplet states, Norrish-Type I and Type II reactions.

7. Spectroscopy

Principle and applications in structure elucidation:

- **Rotational:** Diatomic molecules; isotopic substitution and rotational constants.
- **Vibrational:** Diatomic molecules, linear triatomic molecules, specific frequencies of functional groups in polyatomic molecules.
- **Electronic:** Singlet and triplet states. $n \rightarrow \pi$ p* and $\pi\pi \rightarrow$ p* transitions; application to conjugated double bonds and conjugated carbonyls Woodward-Fieser rules; Charge transfer spectra.
- **Nuclear Magnetic Resonance (1HNMR):** Basic principle; chemical shift and spin-spin interaction and coupling constants.
- **Mass Spectrometry:** Parent peak, base peak, metastable peak, McLafferty rearrangement.

CIVIL ENGINEERING

Paper-I

1. Engineering Mechanics, Strength of Materials and Structural Analysis.

- **Engineering Mechanics:**
  - Units and Dimensions, SI Units, Vectors, Concept of Force, Concept of particle and rigid body. Concurrent, Non-Concurrent and parallel forces in a plane, moment of force free body diagram, conditions of equilibrium, Principle of virtual work, equivalent force system.
  - First and Second Moment of area, Mass moment of Inertia. Static Friction.
  - Kinematics and Kinetics:
  - Kinematics in cartesian Co-ordinates, motion under uniform and non-uniform acceleration, motion under gravity. Kinetics of particle: Momentum and Energy principles, collision of elastic bodies, rotation of rigid bodies.
- **Strength of Materials:**
  - Simple Stress and Strain, Elastic constants, axially loaded compression members, Shear force and bending moment, theory of simple bending, Shear Stress distribution across cross sections, Beams of uniform strength.
  - Deflection of beams: Mecaulay's method, Mohr's Moment area method, Conjugate beam method, unit load method. Torsion of Shafts, Elastic stability of columns, Euler's, Rankine's and Secant formulae.
- **Structural Analysis:**
  - Castiglianio's theorems I and II, unit load method, of consistent deformation applied to beams and pin jointed trusses. Slope-deflection, moment distribution.
  - **Rolling loads and Influences lines:** Influences lines for Shear Force and Bending moment at a section of a beam. Criteria for maximum shear force and bending Moment in beams traversed by a system of moving loads. Influences lines for simply supported plane pin jointed trusses.
  - **Arches:** Three hinged, two hinged and fixed arches, rib shortening and temperature effects.
  - **Matrix mehods of analysis:** Force method and displacement method of analysis of indeterminate beams and rigid frames.

- **Plastic Analysis of beams and frames:** Theory of plastic bending, plastic analysis, statical method, Mechanism method.
- **Unsymmetrical bending:** Moment of inertia, product of inertia, position of Neutral Axis and Principal axes, calculation of bending stresses.

2. Design of Structures: Steel, Concrete and Masonry Structures.

- **Structural Steel Design:**
  - **Structural steel:** Factors of safety and load factors. Riveted, bolted and welded joints and connections. Design of tension and compression members, beams of built up section, riveted and welded plate girders, gantry girders, stancheons with battens and lacings.
- **Design of Concrete and Masonry Structures:**
  - **Concept of mix design. Reinforced Concrete:** Working Stress and Limit State method of design— Recommendations of I. S. codes. Design of one way and two way slabs, stair-case slabs, simple and continuous beams of rectangular, T and L sections. Compression members under direct load with or without eccentricity.
  - Cantilever and Counter fort type retaining walls.
  - **Water tanks:** Design requirements for Rectangular and circular tanks resting on ground.
  - **Prestressed Concrete:** Methods and systems of prestressing, anchorages, Analysis and design of sections for flexure based on working stress, loss of prestress.
  - Design of brick masonry as per I. S. Codes

3. Fluid Mechanics, Open Channel Flow and Hydraulic Machines:

- **Fluid Mechanics:**
  - Fluid properties and their role in fluid motion, fluid statics including forces acting on plane and curve surfaces.
  - Kinematics and Dynamics of Fluid flow: Velocity and accelerations, stream lines, equation of continuity, irrotational and rotational flow, velocity potential and stream functions.
  - Continuity, momentum, energy equation, Navier Stokes equation, Euler's equation of motion, application to fluid flow problems, pipe flow, sluice gates, weirs.

- **Dimensional Analysis and Similitude:** Buckingham's Pi-theorem, dimensionless parameters.
- **Laminar Flow:** Laminar flow between parallel, stationary and moving plates, flow through tube.
- **Boundary layer:**
  - Laminar and turbulent boundary layer on a flat plate, laminar sub-layer, smooth and rough boundaries, drag and lift.
  - Turbulent flow through pipes: Characteristics of turbulent flow, velocity distribution and variation of pipe friction factor, hydraulic grade line and total energy line.
- **Open Channel Flow:** Uniform and non-uniform flows, momentum and energy correction factors, specific energy and specific force, critical depth, rapidly varied flow, hydraulic jump, gradually varied flow, classification of surface profiles, control section, step method of integration of varied flow equation.
- **Hydraulic Machines and Hydropower:**
  - Hydraulic turbines, types classification, Choice of turbines performance parameters, controls, characteristics, specific speed.
  - Principles of hydropower development.

4. Geotechnical Engineering:

- Soil Type and Structure—gradation and particle size distribution—consistency limits.
- Water in soil—capillary and structural—effective stress and pore water pressure—permeability concept—filed and laboratory determination of permeability—Seepage pressure—quick sand conditions—Shear strength determination—Mohr Coulomb concept.
- Compaction of soil—Laboratory and filed test.
- Compressibility and consolidation concept—consolidation theory—consolidation settlement analysis.
- Earth pressure theory and analysis for retaining walls, Application for sheet piles and Braced excavation.
- Bearing capacity of soil—approaches for analysis- Filed tests— settlement analysis—stability of slope of earth walk.
- Subsuface exploration of soils—methods
- Foundation—Type and selection criteria for foundation of structures—Design criteria for foundation—Analysis of distribution of stress for footings and pile—pile group action—pile load test.
- Ground improvement techniques.

Paper – II

1. Construction Technology, Equipment, Planning and Management

- **Construction Technology**
  - Engineering Materials:
  - Physical properties of construction materials with respect to their use in construction—Stones, Bricks and Tiles; Lime, Cement, different types of Mortars and Concrete.
  - Specific use of ferro cement, fibre reinforced C. C., High stength concrete. Timber; Properties defects—common preservation treatments.
  - Use and selection of materials for specific use like Low Cost Housing, Mass Housing, High Rise Buildings.
- **Construction:**
  - Masonry principles using Brick, stone, Blocks—construction detailing and strength characteristics.
  - Types of plastering, pointing, flooring, roofing and construction features. Common repairs in buildings.
  - Principle of functional planning of building for residents and specific use—Building code provisions.
  - Basic principles of detailed and approximate estimating—specification writing and rate analysis-principles of valuation of real property.
  - Machinery for earthwork, concreting and their specific uses—Factors affecting selection of equipments—operating cost of equipments.
- **Construction Planning And Management:**
  - Construction activity—schedules—organization for construction industry—Quality assurance principles.
  - Use Basic principle of network—analysis in form of CPM and PERT their use in construction monitoring, Cost optimization and resource allocation
  - Basic principles of Economic analysis and methods.
  - Project profitability—Basic principles of Boot approach to financial planning-simple toll fixation criterions.

2. Surveying and Transportation Engineering

- **Surveying:** Common methods and instruments for distance and angle measurement for CE work—their use in plane table, traverse survey, levelling work, triangulation, contouring and topographical map.

- Basic principles of photogrammetry and remote sensing.
- **Railways Engineering:** Permanent way—components, types and their function-Functions and Design constituents of turn and crossing— Necessity of geometric design of track—Design of station and yards.
- **Highway Engineering:**
  - Principles of Highway alignments—classification and geometrical design elements and standards for Roads.
  - Pavement structure for flexible and rigid pavements —Design principles and methodology of pavements.
  - Typical construction methods and standards of materials for stabilized soil, WBM, Bituminous works and CC roads.
  - Surface and sub-surface drainge arrangements for roads—culvert structures. Pavement distresses and strengthening by overlays.
  - Traffic surveys and their application in traffic planning—Typical design features for channelized, intersection rotary etc.—signal designs—standard Traffic signs and markings.

3. Hydrology, Water Resources and Engineering:

- **Hydrology:** Hydrological cycle, precipitation, evaporation, transpiration, infiltration, overland flow, hydrograph, flood frequency analyses, flood routing through a reservoir, channel flow routing—Muskingam method.
- **Ground Water flow:** Specific yield, storage coefficient, coefficient of permeability, confined and unconfined aquifers, aquifers, aquitards, radial flow into a well under confined and unconfined conditions.
- **Water Resources Engineering:** Ground and surface water resources, single and multipurpose projects, storage capacity of reservoirs, reservoir losses, reservoir sedimentation.
- **Irrigation Engineering:**
  - **Water requirements of crops:** consumptive use, duty and delta, irrigation methods and their efficiencies.
  - Canals: Distribution systems for cannal irrigation, canal capacity, canal losses, alignment of main and distributory canals, most efficient section, lined canals, their design, regime theory, critical shear stress, bed load.
  - **Water logging:** causes and control, salinity.
  - **Canal structures:** Design of head regulators, canal falls, aqueducts, metering flumes and canal outlets.

- **Diversion head work:** Principles and design of weirs on permeable and impermeable foundation, Khosla's theory, energy dissipation.
- **Storage works:** Types of dams, design, principles of rigid gravity stability analysis.
- **Spillways:** Spillway types, energy dissipation.
- **River training:** Objectives of river training, methods of river training.

4. Environmental Engineering

- **Water Supply:** Predicting demand for water, impurities of water and their significance, physical, chemical and bacteriological analysis, waterborne diseases, standards for potable water.
- **Intake of Water:** Water treatment: principles of coagulation, flocculation and sedimentation; slow-, rapid-, pressure-, filters; chlorination, softening, removal of taste, odour and salinity.
- Sewerage Systems: Domestic and industrial wastes, store sewage—separate and combined systems, flow through sewers, design of sewers.
- **Sewage Characterisation:** BOD, COD, solids, dissolved oxygen, nitrogen and TOC. Standards of disposal in normal water course and on land.
- **Sewage Treatment:** Working principles, units, chambers, sedimentation tank, trickling filters, oxidation ponds, activated sludge process, septic tank, disposal of sludge, recycling of waste water.
- **Solid waste:** Collection and disposal in rural and urban contexts, management of long-term ill-effects.

5. Environmental pollution:

Sustainable development. Radioactive wastes and disposal. Environmental impact assessment for thermal power plants, mines, river valley projects. Air pollution. Pollution control acts.

COMMERCE AND ACCOUNTANCY

Paper-I: Accounting and Finance

Accounting, Taxation & Auditing

1. *Financing Accounting:*

- Accounting as a financial information system; Impact of behavioural sciences. Accounting Standards e.g., Accounting for Depreciation, Inventories, Research and Development Costs, Long-term Construction Contracts, Revenue Recognition, Fixed Assets, Contingencies, Foreign Exchange Transactions, Investments and Government Grants, Cash Flow Statement, Earnings per Share.
- Accounting for Share Capital Transactions including Bonus Shares, Right Shares. Emplyees Stock Option and Buy-Back of Securities.
- Preparation and Presentation of Company Final Accounts. Amalgamations, Absorption and Reconstruction of Companies.

2. *Cost Accounting*

- Nature and functions of cost accounting. Installation of Cost Accounting System. Cost Concepts related to Income Measurement, Profit Planning, Cost Control and Decision Making.
- Methods of Costing: Job Costing, Process Costing, Activity Based Costing. Volume-cost-Profit Relationship as a tool of Profit Planning.
- Incremental Analysis/Differential Costing as a Tool of Pricing Decisions, Product Decisions, Make or Buy Decisions, Shut-Down Decisions etc.
- Techniques of Cost Control and Cost Reduction: Budgeting as a Tool of Planning and Control. Standard Costing and Variance Analysis.
- Responsibility Accounting and Divisional Performance Measurement.

3. *Taxation*

- **Income Tax:** Definitions. Basis of charge; Incomes which do not form part of total income. Simple problems of Computation of Income (of individuals only) under various heads, i.e., Salaries, Income from House Property, Profits and Gains from Business or Profession, Capital Gains, Income from other sources, Income of other Persons included in Assessee's Total Income.
- Set-off and Carry forward of Loss. Deductions from Gross Total Income.
- Salient Features/Provisions Related to VAT and Services Tax.

4. Auditing

- **Company Audit:** Audit related to Divisible Profits, Dividends, Special investigations, Tax audit.
- Audit of Banking, Insurance, Non-Profit Organization and Charitable Societies/ Trusts/Organizations.

Financial Management, Financial Institutions and Markets

1. Financial Management:

- **Finance Function:** Nature, Scope and Objectives of Financial Management: Risk and Return Relationship.
- **Tools of Financial Analysis:** Ratio Analysis, Funds-Flow and Cash-Flow Statement.
- **Capital Budgeting Decisions:** Process, Procedures and Appraisal Methods. Risk and Uncertainty Anlysis and Methods.
- **Cost of Capital:** Concept, Computation of Specific Costs and Weighted Average Cost of Capital. CAPM as aTool of Determining Cost of Equity Capital.
- **Financing Decisions:** Theories of Capital Structure—Net Income (NI) Approach.
- **Net Operating Income (NOI) Approach, MM Approach and Traditional Approach. Designing of Capital structure:** Types of Leverages (Operating, Financial and Combined), EBIT-EPS Analysis, and other Factors.
- **Dividend Decisions and Valuation of Firm:** Walter's Model, MM Thesis, Gordan's Model Lintner's Model. Factors Affecting Dividend Policy.
- **Working Capital Management:** Planning of Working Capital. Determinants of Working Capital. Components of Working Capital—Cash, Inventory and Receivables.
- Corporate Restructuring with focus on Mergers and Acquisitions (Financial aspect only).

2. Financial Markets and Institutions:

- **Indian Financial System:** An Overview
- **Money Markets:** Participants, Structure and Instruments. Commercial Banks. Reforms in Banking Sector. Monetary and Credit Policy of RBI. RBI as a Regulator.
- **Capital Market:** Primary and Secondary Market. Financial Market Instruments and Innovative Debt Instruments; SEBI as a Regulator.
- **Financial Services:** Mutual Funds, Venture Capital, Credit Rating Agencies, Insurance and IRDA.

Paper-II: Organisation Theory and Behaviours, Human Resource Management and Industrial Relations

Organisation Theory and Behaviour

1. *Organisation Theory:*

- Nature and Concept of Organisation; External Environment of Organisation—Technological, Social, Political, Ecomomical and Legal; Organizational Goals Primary and Secondary Goals, Single and Multiple Goals; Management by Objectives.
- Evolution of Organisation theory: Classical Neo-classical and system approach.
- Modern Concepts of Organisation Theory: Organisational Design, Organisational Structure and Organisational Culture.
- Organisational Design—Basic Challenges; Differentiation and Intergration Process; Centralization and Decentralization Process; Standardization/Formalization and Mutual Adjustment. Coordinating Formal and Informal Organizations. Mechanistic and Organic Structures.
- Designing Organizational structures—Authority and Control; Line and Staff Functions, Specialization and Coordination. Types of Organization Structure—Functional. Matrix Structure, Project Structure. Nature and Basis of Power, Sources of Power, Power Structure and Politics. Impact of Information Technology on Organizational Design and Structure.
- Managing Organizational Culture.

2. *Organisation Behaviour:*

- Meaning and Concept; Individual in organization: Personality, Theories, and Determinants; Pereception Meaning and Process.
- Motivation: Concepts, Theories and Applications. Leadership—Theories and Styles. Quality of Work Life (QWL): Meaning and its impact on Performance, Ways of its Enhancement. Quality Circles (QC)—Meaning and their Importance. Management of Conflicts in Organizations. Transactional Analysis, Organizational Effectiveness, Management of Change.

Human Resources Management and Industrial Relations

1. *Human Resources Management (HRM):*

Meaning Nature and Scope of HRM, Human Resource Planning, Job Analysis, Job Description, Job Specification, Recruitment Process, Selection Process,

Orientational and Placement, Training and Development Process, Performance Appraisal and 360° Feed Back, Salary and Wage Administration, Job Evaluation, Employee Welfare, Promotions, Transfers and Separations.

2. Industrial Relations (IR):

- Meaning, Nature, Importance and Scope of IR, Formation of Trade Union, Trade Union Legislation, Trade Union Movement in India. Recognition of Trade Unions, Problems of Trade Unions in India. Impact of Liberalization on Trade Union Movement.
- Nature of Industrial Disputes: Strikes and Lockouts, Causes of Disputes, Prevention and Settlement of Disputes.
- Worker's Participation in Management: Philosophy, Rationale, Present Day Status and Future Prospects.
- Adjudication and Collective Bargaining.
- Industrial Relations in Public Enterprises Absenteeism and Labour Turnover in Indian Industries and their Causes and Remedies.
- ILO and its Functions.

ECONOMICS

Paper – I

1. Advanced Micro Economics:

- Marshallian and Varrasiam Approaches to Price determination.
- Alternative Distribution Theories; Ricardo, Kaldor, Kaleeki.
- Markets Structure: Monopolistic Competition, Duopoly, Oligopoly.
- Modern Welfare Criteria: Pareto Hicks and Scitovsky, Arrow's Impossibility Theorem, A. K. Sen's Social Welfare Function.

2. Advance Macro Economics

Approaches to Employment Income and Interest Rate determination: Classical, Keynes (IS)-LM) curve, Neo-classical synthesis and New classical, Theories of Interest Rate determination and Interest Rate Structure.

3. Money-Banking and Finance:

- Demand for and Supply of Money: Money Multiplier Quantity Theory of Money (Fisher, Pique and Friedman) and Keyne's Theory on Demand for Money, Goals and Instruments of Monetary Management in Closed and Open Economies. Relation between the Central Bank and the Treasury. Proposal for ceiling on growth rate of money.
- Public Finance and its Role in market Economy: In stabilisation of supply, allocative, of resources and in distribution and development. Sources of Government revenue, forms of Taxes and Subsidies, their incidence and effects. Limits to taxation, loans, crowding-out effects and limits to borrowings. Public expenditure and its effects.

4. International Economics

- Old and New theories of International Trade.
  - Comparative advantage,
  - Terms of Trade and Offer Curve.
  - Product Cycle and Strategic Trade Theories.
  - Trade as an engine of growth and theories of underdevelopment in an open economy.
- **Forms of Protection:** Tariff and quota.

- **Balance of Payments Adjustment:** Alternative Approaches.
  - Price versus income, income adjustments under fixed exchange rates.
  - Theories of Policy Mix.
  - Exchange rate adjustments under capital mobility.
  - Floating Rates and their Implications for Developing Countries: Currency Boards.
  - Trade Policy and Developing Countries.
  - BOP, adjustments and Policy Coordination in open economy macromodel.
  - Speculative attacks.
  - Trade Blocks and Monetary Unions.
  - WTO: TRIMS, TRIPS, Domestic Measures, Different Rounds of WTO talks.

5. Growth and Development:

- Theories of growth: Harrod's model;
- Lewis model of development with surplus labour.
- Balanced Unbalanced Growth.
- Human Capitals and Economic Growth.
- Research and Development and Economic Growth.
- Process of Economic Development of less developed courtries: Myrdal and Kuzments on economic development and structural change: Role of Agriculture in Economic Development of less developed countries.
- Economic Development and International Trade and Investment, Role of Multinationals.
- Planning and Economic Development: changing role of Markets and Planning, Private-Public Partnership.
- Welfare indicators and measures of growth—Human Development Indices. The basic needs approach.
- Development and Environmental Sustainability—Renewable and Non-renewable Resources, Environmental Degradation, Intergenerational equity development.

Paper-II

1. Indian Economics in Post-Independence Era:

Land System and its changes, Commercialization of agriculture Drain theory, Laissez faire theory and critique. Manufacture and Transport: Jute, Cotton, Railways, Money and Credit.

2. Indian Economy after Independence:

- The Pre-Liberalization Era:
  - Contribution of Vakil, Gadgil and V.K.R.V. Rao.
  - Agricultrure: Land Reforms and land tenure system, Green Revolution and capital formation in agriculture.
  - Industry Trends in composition and growth, Role of public and private sector, small scale and cottage industries.
  - National and Per capita income: Patterns, trends, aggregate and sectoral composition and changes therein.
  - Broad factors determining National Income and distribution, Measures of poverty, Trends in poverty and inequality.
- **The Post-Liberalization Era:**
  - **New Economic Reform and Agriculture:** Agriculture and WTO, Food processing, subsidies, Agricultural prices and public distribution system, Impact of public expenditure on agricultural growth.
  - **New Economic Policy and Industry:** Strategy of industrialization, Privatization, Disinvestments, Role of foreign direct investment and multinationals.
  - **New Economic Policy and Trade:** Intellectual property rights: Implications of TRIPS, TRIMS, GATS and new EXIM policy.
  - **New Exchange Rate Regime:** Partial and full convertibility, Capital account convertibility.
  - **New Economic Policy and Public Finance:** Fiscal Responsibility Act, Twelfth Finance Commission and Fiscal Federalism and Fiscal Consolidation.
  - New Economic Policy and Monetary System. Role of RBI under the new regime.
  - **Planning:** From central Planning to indivative planning, Relation between planning and markets for growth and decentralized planning: 73rd and 74th Constitutional amendments.
  - **New Economic Policy and Employment:** Employment and poverty, Rural wages, Employment Generation, Poverty alleviation schemes, New Rural, Employment Guarantee Scheme.

ELECTRICAL ENGINEERING

Paper-I

1. Circuits – Theory:

Circuit components; network graphs; KCL, KVL; Circuit analysis methods: nodal analysis, mesh analysis; basic network theorems and applications; transient analysis: RL, RC and RLC circuits; sinusoidal steady state analysis; resonant circuits; coupled circuits; balanced 3-phase circuits. Two-port networks.

2. Signals and Systems:

Representation of continuous-time and discrete-time signals and systems; LTI systems; convolution; impulse response; time-domain analysis of LTI systems based on convolution and differential/difference equations. Fourier transform, Laplace transform, Z-transform, Transfer function. Sampling and recovery of signals DFT, FFT Processing of analog signals through discrete-time systems.

3. E.M. Theory

Maxwell's equations, wave propagation in bounded media. Boundary conditions, reflection and refraction of plane waves. Transmission lines: travelling and standing waves, ipedance matching, Smith chart.

4. Analog Electronics

Characteristics and equivalent circuits (large and small-signal) of Diode, BJT, JFET and MOSFET. Diode circuits: Clipping, clamping, rectifier. Biasing and bias stability. FET amplifiers. Current mirror; Amplifiers: single and multi-stage, differential, operational feedback and power. Analysis of amplifiers; frequency-response of amplifiers. OPAMP circuits. Filters; sinusoidal oscillators: criterion for oscillation; single-transistor and OPAMP configurations. Function generators and wave-shaping circuits. Linear and switching power supplies.

5. Digital Electronics

Boolean algebra; minimisation of Boolean functions; logic gates; digital IC families (DTL, TTL, ECL, MOS, CMOS). Combinational circuits: arithmetic circuits, code converters, multiplexers and decoders. Sequential circuits: latches and flip-flops, counters and shift-registers. Comparators, timers, multivibrators. Sample and hold circuits, ADCs and DACs. Semiconductor memories. Logic implementation using programmable devices (ROM, PLA, FPGA).

6. Energy Conversion

Principles of electromechanical energy conversion: Torque and emf in rotating machines. DC machines: characteristics and performance analysis; starting and speed control of motors. Transformers: principles of operation and analysis; regulation, efficiency; 3-phase transformers. 3-phase induction machines and synchronous machines: characteristics and performance analysis; speed control.

7. Power Electronics and Electric Drives

Semi-conductor power devices: diode, transistor, thyristor, triac, GTO and MOSFET-static characteristics and principles of operation; triggering circuits; phase control rectifiers; bridge converters: fully-controlled and half-controlled; principles of thyristor choppers and inverters; DC-DC converters; Switch mode inverter; basic concepts of speed control of dc and ac motor drives applications of variable-speed drives.

8. Analog Communication

Random variables: continuous, discrete; probability, probability functions. Statistical averages; probability models; Random signals and noise: white noise, noise equivalent bandwidth; signal transmission with noise; signal to noise ratio. Linear CW modulation: Amplitude modulation: DSB, DSB-SC and SSB. Modulators and Demodulators; Phase and Frequency modulation: PM & FM signals; narrows band FM; generation & detection of FM and PM, Deemphasis, Preemphasis. CW modulation system: Superhetrodyne receivers, AM receivers, communication receivers, FM receivers, phase locked loop, SSB receiver Signal to noise ratio calculation or AM and FM receivers.

Paper–II

1. Control Systems

Elements of control systems; block-diagram representations; open-loop & closed-loop systems; principles and applications of feed-back. Control system components. LTI systems: time-domain and transform-domain analysis. Stability: Routh Hurwitz criterion, root-loci, Bode-plots and polor plots, Nyquist's criterion; Design of lead-lad compensators. Proportional, PI, PID controllers. State-variable representation and analysis of control systems.

2. Microprocessors and Microcomputers

PC organisation; CPU, instruction set, register settiming diagram, programming, interrupts, memory interfacing, I/O interfacing, programmable peripheral devices.

3. Measurement and Instrumentation

Error analysis; measurement of current voltage, power, energy, power-factor, resistance, inductance, capacitance and frequency; bridge measurements. Signal conditioning circuit; Electronic measuring instruments: multimeter, CRO, digital voltmeter, frequency counter, Q-meter, spectrum-analyser, distoration-meter. Transducers: thermocouple, thermistor, LVDT, strain-guage, piezo-electric crystal.

4. Power Systems: Analysis and Control

Steady-state performance of overhead transmission lines and cables; principles of active and reactive power transfer and distribution; per-unit quantities; bus admittance and impedance matrices; load flow; voltage control and power factor correction; economic operation; symmetrical components, analysis of symmetrical and unsymmetrical faults. Concepts of system stability: swing curves and equal area criterion. Static VAR system. Basic concepts of HVDC transmission.

5. Power System Protection:

Principles of overcurrent, differential and distance protection. Concept of solid state relays. Circuit brakers. Computer aided protection: introduction; line, bus, generator, transformer protection; numeric relays and application of DSP to protection.

6. Digital Communication:

Pulse code modulation (PCM), defferential pulse code modulation (DPCM), delta modulation (DM), Digital modulation and demodulation schemes: amplitude, phase and frequency keying schemes (ASK, PSK, FSK). Error control coding: error detection and correction, linear block codes, convolation codes. Information measure and source coding. Data networks, 7-layer architecture.

GEOGRAPHY

Paper–I: Principles of Geography

Physical Geography

- **Geomorphology:** Factors controlling landform development; endogenetic and exogenetic forces; Origin and evolution of the earth's crusts; Fundamentals of geomagnetism; Physical conditions of the earth's interior; Geosynclines; Continental drift; Isostasy; Plate tectonics; Recent views on mountain building; Volcanicity; Earthquakes and Tsunamis; Concepts of geomorphic cycles and Land scape development; Denudation chronology; Channel morphology; Erosion surfaces; Slope development; Applied Geomorphology; Geomorphology, economic geology and environment.
- **Climatology:** Temperature and pressure belts of the world; Heat budget of the earth; Atmospheric circulation; Atmospheric stability and instability. Planetary and local winds; Monsoons and jet streams; Air masses and fronto; Temperate and tropical cyclones; Types and distribution of precipitation; Weather and Climate; Koppen's Thornthwaite's and Trewar Tha's classification of world climate; Hydrological cycle; Global climatic change, and role and response of man in climatic changes Applied climatology and Urban climate.
- **Oceanography:** Bottom topography of the Atlantic, Indian and Pacific Oceans; Temperature and salinity of the oceans; Heat and salt budgets, Ocean deposits; Waves, currents and tides; Marine resources; biotic, mineral and energy resources; Coral reefs coral bleaching; Sea-level changes; Law of the sea and marine pollution.
- **Biogeography:** Genesis of soils; Classification and distribution of soils; Soil profile; Soil erosion, Degrada-tion and conservation; Factors influencing world distribution of plants and animals; Problems of deforestation and conservation measures; Social forestry, agro-forestry; Wild life; Major gene pool centres.
- **Environmental Geography:** Principle ecology; Human ecological adaptations; Influence of man on ecology and environment; Global and regional ecological changes and imbalances; Ecosystem their management and conservation; Environmental degradation, management and conservation; Biodiversity and sustainable development; Environmental policy; Environmental hazards and remedial measures; Environmental education and legislation.

Human Geography

- **Perspectives in Human Geography:** Areal differentiation; Regional synthesis; Dichotomy and dualism; Environmentalism; Quantitative revolution and locational analysis; Radical, behavioural, human and welfare approaches; Languages, religions and secularisation; Cultural regions of the world; Human development indix.
- **Economic Geography:** World economic development: measurement and problems; World resources and their distribution; Energy crisis; the limits to growth; World agriculture: typology of agricultural regions; Agricultural inputs and productivity; Food and nutritions problems; Food security; famine: causes, effects and remedies; World industries: location patterns and problems; Patterns of world trade.
- **Population and Settlement Geography:** Growth and distribution of world population; Demographic attributes; Causes and consequences of migration; Concepts of over-under-and optimum population; Population theories, world population problems and policies, Social well-being and quality of life; Population as social capital.
    - Types and patterns of rural settlements; Environmental issues in rural settlements; Hierarchy of urban settlements; Urban morphology; Concept of primate city and rank-size rule; Functional classification of towns; Sphere of urban influence; Rural-urban fringe; Satellite towns; Problems and remedies of urbanization; Sustainable development of cities.
- **Regional Planning:** Concept of a region; Types of regions and methods of regionalisation; Growth centres and growth poles; Regional imbalances; Regional development strategies; Environmental issues in regional planning; Planning for sustainable development.
- **Models, Theories and Laws in Human Geography:** System analysis in Human geography; Malthusian, Marxian and demographic transition models; Central Place theories of Christaller and Losch; Perroux and Boudeville; Von Thunen's model of agricultural location; Weber's model of industrial location; Ostov's model of stages of growth. Heart-land and Rimland theories; Laws of international boundaries and frontiers.

Paper–II: Geography of India

- **Physical Setting:** Space relationship of India with neighbouring countries; Structure and relief; Drainage system and watersheds; Physiographic regions;

Mechanism of Indian monsoons and rainfall patterns; Tropical cyclones and western disturbances; Floods and droughts; Climatic regions; Natural vegetation, Soil types and their distributions.

- **Resources:** Land, surface and ground water, energy, minerals, biotic and marine resources, Forest and wild life resources and their conservation; Energy crisis.
- **Agriculture:** Infrastructure: irrigation, seeds, fertilizers, power; Institutional factors; land holdings, land tenure and land reforms; Cropping pattern, agricultural productivity, agricultural intensity, crop combination, land capability; Agro and social-forestry; Green revolution and its socio-economic and ecological implications; Significance of dry farming; Livestock resources and white revolution; Aqua-culture; Sericulture, Agriculture and poultry; Agricultural regionalisation; Agro-climatic zones; Agro-ecological regions.
- **Industry:** Evolution of industries; Locational factors of cotton, jute, textile, iron and steel, aluminium, fertiliser, paper, chemical and pharmaceutical, automobile, cottage and ago-based industries; Industrial houses and complexes including public sector underkings; Industrial regionalisation; New industrial policy; Multinationals and liberalisation; Special Economic Zones; Tourism including ecotourism.
- **Transport, Communication and Trade:** Road, railway, waterway, airway and pipeline net works and their complementary roles in regional development; Growing importance of ports on national and foreign trade; Trade balance; Trade Policy;Export processing zones; Developments in communication and information technology and their impacts on economy and society; Indian space programme.
- **Cultural Setting:** Historical Perspective of Indian Society; Racial linguistic and ethnic diversities; religious minorities; Major tribes, tribal areas and their problems; Cultural regions; Growth, distribution and density of population; Demographic attributes: sex-ratio, age structure, literacy rate, work-force, dependency ratio, longevity; migration (inter-regional, interaregional and international) and associated problems; Population problems and policies; Health indicators.
- **Settlements:** Types, patterns and morphology of rural settlements; Urban developments; Morphology of Indian cities; Functional classification of Indian cities; Conurbations and metropolitan regions; Urban sprawl; Slums and asssociated problems; Town planning; Problems of urbanisation and remedies.
- **Regional Development and Planning:** Experience of regional planning in India; Five Year Plans; Integrated rural development programmes; Panchayati Raj and decentralised planning; Command area development; Watershed management;

Planning for backward area, desert, drought-prone, hill tribal area development; Multi-level planning; Regional planning and development of island territories.

- **Political Aspects:** Geographical basis of Indian federalism; State reorganisation; Emergence of new states; Regional consciousness and inter-state issues; International boundary of India and related issues; Cross-border terrorism; India's role in world affairs; Geopolitics of South Asia and Indian Ocean realm.
- **Contemporary Issues:** Ecological issues: Environmental hazards: landslides, earthquakes, Tsunamis, floods and droughts, epidemics; Issues related to environmental pollution; Changes in patterns of land use; Principles of environmental impact assessment and environmental management; Population explosion and food security; Environmental degradation; Deforestation, desertification and soil erosion; Problems of agrarian and industrial unrest; Regional disparities in economic development; Concept of sustainable growth and development; Environmental awareness; Linkage of rivers; Globalisation and Indian economy.

NOTE: Candidates will be required to answer one compulsory map question pertinent to subjects covered by this paper.

GEOLOGY

Paper-I

- **General Geology:** The Solar System, meteorites, origin and interior of the earth and age of earth; Volcanoes—causes and products, Volcanic belts. Earthquakes—causes, effects, seismic of zone of India; Island arcs, trenches and mid-ocean ridges; Continental drift; Seafloor spreading, plate tectonics. Isostasy.
- **Geomorphology and Remote Sensing:** Basic concepts of geomorphology. Weathering and soil formations; Landforms, slopes and drainage. Geomorphic cycles and their interpretation. Morphology and its relation to structures and lithology; Coastal geomorphology; Applications of geomorphology in mineral prospecting, civil engineering; hydrology and environmental studies; Geomorphology of Indian sub-continent.
    - Aerial photographs and their interpretation—merits and limitations; The Electromagnetic spectrum. Orbiting
    - Satellites and Sensor Systems. Indian Remote Sensing Satellites. Satellite data products; Applications of remote sensing in geology; The Geographic Information System (GIS) and Global Positioning System (GPS)—its applications.
- **Structural Geology:** Principles of geologic mapping and map reading, projection diagrams, Stress and strain ellipsoid and stress-strain relationships of elastic, plastic and viscous materials; Strain markers in deformed rocks. Behaviour of minerals and rocks under deformation conditions. Folds and faults classification and mechanics; Structural analysis of folds, foliations, lineations, joints and faults, unconformities; Time-relationship between crystallization and deformation.
- **Paleontology:** Species—definition and nomenclature; Megafossils and Microfossils. Modes of preservation of fossils; Different kinds of microfossils; Application of microfossils in correlation, petroleum exploration, paleoclimatic and paleoceanographic studies; Evolutionary trend in Hominidae, Equidae and Proboscidae. Siwalik fauna.
    - Gondwana flora and fauna and its importance; Index fossils and their significance.
- **Indian Stratigraphy:** Classification of stratigraphic sequences: lithostrati-graphic, biostratigraphic, chrono-stratigraphic and magnetostratigraphic and their interrelationships; Distribution and classification of Precambrian rocks of India; Study of stratigraphic distribution and lithology of Phanerozoic rocks of India with reference to fauna, flora and economic importance. Major boundary

problems—Cambrian/ Precambrian, Permian/Triassic, Cretaceous/Tertiary and Pliocene/Pleistocene; Study of climatic conditions, paleogeography and igneous activity in the Indian sub-continent in the geological past. Tectonic framework of India. Evolution of the Himalayas.

- **Hydrogeology and Engineering Geology:** Hydrologic cycle and genetic classification of water; Movement of subsurface water; Springs; Porosity, permeability, hydraulic conductivity, transmissivity and storage coefficient, classification of aquifers; Water-bearing characteristics of rocks; Groundwater chemistry. Salt water intrusion. Types of wells. Drainage basin morphometry; Exploration for groundwater; Groundwater recharge; Problems and management of groundwater; Rainwater harvesting; Engineering properties of rocks; Geological investigations for dams, tunnels highways, railway and bridges; Rock as construction material; Landslides causes, prevention and rehabilitation; Earthquake-resistant structures.

Paper-II

1. Mineralogy

- Classification of crystals into systems and classes of symmetry; International system of crystallographic notation; Use of projection diagrams to represent crystal symmetry; Elements of X-ray crystallography.
- Physical and chemical characters of rock forming silicate mineral groups; Structural classification of silicates; Common minerals of igneous and metamorphic rocks; Minerals of the carbonate, phosphate, sulphide and halide groups; Clay minerals.
- Optical properties of common rock forming minerals; Pleochroism, extinction angle, double refraction, birefringence, twinning and dispersion in minerals.

2. Igneous and Metamorphic Petrology

- Generation and crystallisation of magmas. Crystallisation of albite—anorthite, diopside—anorthite and diopside—wollastonite—silica systems. Bowen's Reaction Principle; Magmatic differentiation and assimilation. Petrogenetic significance of the textures and structures of igneous rocks. Petrography and petrogenesis of granite, syenite, diorite, basic and ultrabasic groups, charnockite, anorthosite and alkaline rocks. Carbonatites. Deccan volcanic province.
- Types and agents of metamorphism. Metamorphic grades and zones; Phase rule. Facies of regional and contact metamorphism; ACF and AKF diagrams; Textures

and structures of metamorphic rocks. Metamorphism of arenaceous, argillaceous and basic rocks; Minerals assemblages. Retrograde metamorphism; Metasomatism and granitisation, migmatites. Granulite terrains of India.

3. Sedimenary Petrology

Sedimentas and Sedimentary rocks: Processes of formation; digenesis and lithification; Clastic and non-clastic rocks-their classification, petrography and depositional environment; Sedimentary facies and provenance. Sedimentary structures and their significance. Heavy minerals and their significance. Sedimentary basins of India.

4. Economic Geology

Ore, ore mineral and gangue, tenor of ore. Classification of ore deposits; Processes of formation of mineral deposits; Controls of ore localisation; Ore texures and structures; Metallogenic epochs and provinces; Geology of the important Indian deposits of aluminium, chromium, copper, gold, iron, lead, zinc, manganese, titanium, uranium and thorium and industrial minerals; Deposits of coal and petroleum in India, National Mineral Policy; Conservation and utilization of mineral resources. Marine mineral resources and Law of Sea.

5. Mining Geology

Methods of prospecting—geological, geophysical, geochemical and geobotanical; Techniques of sampling. Estimation of reserves of ore; Methods of exploration and mining-metallic ores, industrial minerals, marine mineral resources and building stones. Mineral beneficiation and ore dressing.

6. Geochemistry and Environmental Geology

- Cosmic abundance of elements. Composition of the planets and meteorites. Structure and composition of earth and distribution of elements. Trace elements. Elements of crystal chemistry-types of chemical bonds, coordination number. Isomorphism and polymorphism. Elementary thermodynamics.
- Natural hazards—floods, mass wasting, costal hazards, earthquakes and volcanic activity and mitigation; Environmental impact of urbanization, mining, industrial and radioactive waste disposal, use of fertilizers, dumping of mine waste and fly-ash. Pollution of ground and surface water, marine pollution. Environment protection—legislative measures in India; Sea level changes: causes and impact.

HISTORY

Paper–I

1. Sources

- **Archaeological sources:**
  - Exploration, excavation, epigraphy, numismatics, monuments. Literary sources:
  - Indigenous: Primary and secondary; poetry, scientific literature, literature, literature in regional languages, religious literature.
  - Foreign account: Greek, Chinese and Arab writers.

2. Pre-history and Proto-history

Geographical factors; hunting and gathering (paleolithic and mesolithic); Beginning of agriculture (neolithic and chalcolithic).

3. Indus Valley Civilization

Origin, date, extent, characteristics-decline, survival and significance, art and architecture.

3. Megalithic Cultures

Distribution of pastoral and farming cultures outside the Indus, Development of community life, Settlements, Development of agriculture, Crafts, Pottery, and Iron industry.

4. Aryans and Vedic Period

Expansions of Aryans in India: Vedic Period: Religious and philosophic literature; Transformation from Rig Vedic period to the later Vedic period; Political, social and economical life; Significance of the Vedic Age; Evolution of Monarchy and Varna system.

5. Period of Mahajanapadas

- Formation of States (Mahajanapada): Republics and monarchies; Rise of urban centres; Trade routes; Economic growth; Introduction of coinage; Spread of Jainism and Buddhism; Rise of Magadha and Nandas.
- Iranian and Mecedonian invasions and their impact.

6. Mauryan Empire

Foundation of the Mauryan Empire, Chandragupta, Kautilya and Arthashastra; Ashoka; Concept of Dharma; Edicts; Polity, Administration, Economy; Art, architecture and sculpture; External contacts; Religion; Spread of religion; Literature. Disintegration of the empire; sungas and Kanvas.

7. Post-Mauryan Period (Indo-Greeks, Sakas, Kushanas, Western Kshatrapas)

Contact with outside world; growth of urban centres, economy, coinage, development of religions, Mahayana, social conditions, art, architecture, culture, literature and science.

8. Early State and Society in Eastern India, Deccan and South India

Kharavela, The Satavahanas, Tamil States of the Sangam Age; Administration, Economy, land grants, coinage, trade guilds and urban centres; Buddhist centres; Sangam literature and culture; Art and architecture.

9. Guptas, Vakatakas and Vardhanas

Polity and administration, Economic conditions, Coinage of the Guptas, Land grants, Decline of urban centres, Indian feudalism, Caste system, Position of women, Education and educational institutions; Nalanda, Vikramshila and Vallabhi, Literature, scientific literature, art and architecture.

10. Regional States during Gupta Era

The Kadambas, Pallavas, Chalukyas of Badami; Polity and Administration, Trade guilds, Literature; growth of Vaishnava and Saiva religions. Tamil Bhakit movement, Shankaracharya; Vedanta; Institutions of temple and temple architecture; Palas, Senas, Rashtrakutas, Paramaras, Polity and administration; Cultural aspects. Arab conquest of Sind; Alberuni, The Chaluky as of Kalyana, Cholas, Hoysalas, Pandyas; Polity and Administration; Local Government; Growth of art and architecture, religious sects, Institution of temple and Mathas, Agraharas, education and literature, economy and society.

11. Themes in Early Indian Cultural History

Languages and texts, major stages in the evolution of art and architecture, major philosophical thinkers and schools, ideas in Science and Mathematics.

12. Early Medieval India, 750-1200

- **Polity:** Major political developments in Northern India and the peninsula, origin and the rise of Rajputs.
- **The Cholas:** administration, village economy and society "Indian Feudalism".
- Agrarian economy and urban settlements.
- Trade and commerce.
- **Society:** the status of the Brahman and the new social order.
- Condition of women.
- Indian science and technology.

13. Cultural Traditions in India, 750-1200

- **Philosophy:** Skankaracharya and Vedanta, Ramanuja and Vishishtadvaita, Madhva and Brahma-Mimansa.
- **Religion:** Forms and features of religion, Tamil devotional cult, growth of Bhakti, Islam and its arrival in India, Sufism.
- **Literature:** Literature in Sanskrit, growth of Tamil literature, literature in the newly developing languages, Kalhan's Rajtarangini, Alberuni's India.
- Art and Architecture: Temple architecture, sculpture, painting.

14. The Thirteenth Century

- **Establishment of the Delhi Sultanate:** The Ghurian invasions - factors behind Ghurian success.
- Economic, Social and cultural consequences.
- Foundation of Delhi Sultanate and early Turkish Sultans.
- Consolidation: The rule of Iltutmish and Balban.

15. The Fourteenth Century

- "The Khalji Revolution".
- Alauddin Khalji: Conquests and territorial expansion, agrarian and economic measure.
- Muhammad Tughluq: Major projects, agrarian measures, bureaucracy of Muhammad Tughluq.
- Firuz Tugluq: Agrarian measures, achievements in civil engineering and public works, decline of the Sultanate, foreign contacts and Ibn Battuta's account.

16. Society, Culture and Economy in the Thirteenth and Fourteenth Centuries

- Society: composition of rural society, ruling classes, town dwellers, women, religious classes, caste and slavery under the Sultanate, Bhakti movement, Sufi movement.
- Culture: Persian literature, literature in the regional languages of North India, literaute in the languages of South India, Sultanate architecture and new structural forms, painting, evolution of a composite culture.
- Economy: Agricultural Production, rise of urban economy and non-agricultural production, trade and commerce.

17. The Fifteenth and Early Sixteenth Century-Political Developments and Economy

- Rise of Provincial Dynasties: Bengal, Kashmir (Zainul Abedin), Gujarat.
- Malwa, Bahmanids.
- The Vijayanagara Empire.
- Lodis.
- Mughal Empire, first phase: Babur, Humayun.
- The Sur Empire: Sher Shah's administration.
- Portuguese colonial enterprise, Bhakti and Sufi Movements.

18. The Fifteenth and Early Sixteenth Century- Society and culture

- Regional cultures specificities.
- Literary traditions.
- Provincial architectural.
- Society, culture, literature and the arts in Vijayanagara Empire.

19. Akbar

- Conquests and consolidation of empire.
- Establishment of *jagir* and *mansab* systems.
- Rajput policy.
- Evolution of religious and social outlook. Theory of *Sulh-i-kul* and religious policy.
- Court patronage of art and technology.

20. Mughal Empire in the Seventeenth Century

- Major administrative policies of Jahangir, Shahjahan and Aurangzeb.
- The Empire and the Zamindars.
- Religious policies of Jahangir, Shahjahan and Aurangzeb.
- Nature of the Mughal State.
- Late Seventeenth Century crisis and the revolts.
- The Ahom kingdom.
- Shivaji and the early Maratha Kingdom.

21. Economy and society, in the 16th and 17th Centuries

- Population Agricultural and craft production.
- Towns, commerce with Europe through Dutch, English and French companies: a trade revolution.
- Indian mercantile classes. Banking, insurance and credit systems.
- Conditions of peasants, Condition of Women.
- Evolution of the Sikh community and the Khalsa Panth.

22. Culture during Mughal Empire

- Persian histories and other literature.
- Hindi and religious literatures.
- Mughal architecture.
- Mughal painting.
- Provincial architecture and painting.
- Classical music.
- Science and technology.

23. The Eighteenth Century

- Factors for the decline of the Mughal Empire.
- The regional principalities: Nizam's Deccan, Bengal, Awadh.
- Maratha ascendancy under the Peshwas.
- The Maratha fiscal and financial system.
- Emergence of Afghan power Battle of Panipat, 1761.
- State of, political, cultural and economic, on eve of the British conquest.

Paper-II

1. European Penetration into India

The Early European Settlements; The Portuguese and the Dutch; The English and the French East India Companies; Their struggle for supremacy; Carnatic Wars; Bengal-The conflict between the English and the Nawabs of Bengal; Siraj and the English; The Battle of Plassey; Significance of Plassey.

2. British Expansion in India

Bengal-Mir Jafar and Mir Kasim; The Battle of Buxar; Mysore; The Marathas; The three Anglo-Maratha Wars; The Punjab.

3. Early Structure of the British Raj

The Early administrative structure; From diarchy to direct contol; The Regulating Act (1773); The Pitt's India Act (1784); The Charter Act (1833); The Voice of free trade and the changing character of British colonial rule; The English utilitarian and India.

4. Economic Impact of British Colonial Rule

- Land revenue settlements in British India; The Permanent Settlement; Ryotwari Settlement; Mahalwari Settlement; Economic impact of the revenue arrangements; Commercialization of agriculture; Rise of landless agrarian labourers; Impoverishment of the rural society.
- Dislocation of traditional trade and commerce; De-industrialisation; Decline of traditional crafts; Drain of wealth; Economic transformation of India; Railroad and communication network including telegraph and postal services; Famine and poverty in the rural interior; European business enterprise and its limitations.

5. Social and Cultural Developments:

The state of indigenous education, its dislocation; Orientalist-Anglicist controversy, The introduction of western education in India; The rise of press, literature and public opinion; The rise of modern vernacular literature; Progress of Science; Christian missionary activities in India.

6. Social and Religious Reform Movements in Bengal and Other Areas

Ram Mohan Roy, The Brahmo Movement; Devendranath Tagore; Iswarchandra Vidyasagar; The Young Bengal Movement; Dayanada Saraswati; The social reform movements in India including Sati, widow remarriage, child marriage etc.; The contribution of Indian renaissance to the growth of modern India; Islamic revivalism- the Feraizi and Wahabi Movements.

7. Indian Response to British Rule

- Peasant movement and tribal uprisings in the 18th and 19th centuries including the Rangpur Dhing (1783), the Kol Rebellion (1832), the Mopla Rebellion in Malabar (1841-1920), the Santal Hul (1855), Indigo Rebellion (1859-60), Deccan Uprising (1875) and the Munda Ulgulan (1899-1900); The Great Revolt of 1857 —Origin, character, casuses of failure, the consequences; The shift in the character of peasant uprisings in the post-1857 period; the peasant movements of the 1920s and 1930s.
- Factors leading to the birth of Indian Nationalism; Politics of Association; The Foundation of the Indian National Congress; The Safety-valve thesis relating to the birth of the Congress; Programme and objectives of Early Congress; the social composition of early Congress leadership; the Moderates and Extremists; The Partition of Bengal (1905); The Swadeshi Movement in Bengal; the economic and political aspects of Swadeshi Movement; The beginning of revolutionary extremism in India.
- Rise of Gandhi; Character of Gandhian nationalism; Gandhi's popular appeal; Rowlatt Satyagraha; the Khilafat Movement; the Non-cooperation Movement; National politics from the end of the Non-cooperation movement to the beginning of the Civil Disobedience Movement; the two phases of the Civil Disobedience Movement; Simon Commission; The Nehru Report; the Round Table Conferences; Nationalism and the Peasant Movements; Nationalism and Working class movements; Women and Indian youth and students in Indian politics (1885-1947); the election of 1937 and the formation of ministries; Cripps Mission; the Quit India Movement; the Wavell Plan; The Cabinet Mission.
- Constitutional Developments in the Colonial India between 1858 and 1935.
- Other strands in the National Movement.
- The Revolutionaries: Bengal, the Punjab, Maharashtra, U.P. the Madras Presidency, Outside India.
- The Left; The Left within the Congress: Jawaharlal Nehru, Subhas Chandra Bose, the Congress Socialist Party; the Communist Party of India, other left parties.
- Politics of Separatism; the Muslim League; the Hindu Mahasabha; Communalism and the politics of partition; Transfer of power; Independence.
- Consolidation as a Nation; Nehru's Foreign Policy; India and her neighbours (1947-1964); The linguistic reorganisation of States (1935-1947); Regionalism

and regional inequality; Integration of Princely States; Princes in electoral politics; the Question of National Language.

- Caste and Ethnicity after 1947; Backward Castes and Tribes in post-colonial electoral politics; Dalit movements.
- Economic development and political change; Land reforms; the politics of planning and rural reconstruction; Ecology and environmental policy in post-colonial India; Progress of Science.

1. Enlightenment and Modern ideas

- Major Ideas of Enlightenment: Kant, Rousseau.
- Spread of Enlightenment in the colonies.
- Rise of socialist ideas (up to Marx); spread of Marxian Socialism.

2. Origins of Modern Politics

- European States System.
- American Revolution and the Constitution.
- French Revolution and Aftermath, 1789-1815.
- American Civil War with reference to Abraham Lincoln and the abolition of slavery.
- British Democratic politics, 1815-1850: Parliamentary Reformers, Free Traders, Chartists.

3. Industrialization

- English Industrial Revolution: Causes and Impact on Society.
- Industrialization in other countries: USA, Germany, Russia, Japan.
- Industrialization and Globalization.

4. Nation-State System

- Rise of Nationalism in 19th century.
- Nationalism: State-building in Germany and Italy.
- Disintegration of Empires in the face of the emergence of nationalities across the World.

5. Imperialism and Colonialism

- South and South-East Asia.
- Latin America and South Africa.
- Australia.
- Imperialism and free trade: Rise of neo-imperialism.

6. Revolution and Counter-Revolution

- 19th Century European revolutions.
- The Russian Revolution of 1917-1921.
- Fascist Counter-Revolution, Italy and Germany.
- The Chinese Revolution of 1949.

7. World Wars

- 1st and 2nd World Wars as Total Wars: Societal implications.
- **World War I:** Causes and Consequences.
- **World War II:** Causes and Consequences.

8. The World after World War II

- Emergence of Two power blocs.
- Emergence of Third World and non-alignment.
- UNO and the global disputes.

9. Liberation from Colonial Rule

- Latin America-Bolivar.
- Arab World-Egypt.
- Africa-Apartheid to Democracy. South-East Asia-Vietnam.

10. Decolonization and Underdevelopment

Factors constraining Development ; Latin America, Africa.

11. Unification of Europe

- Post War Foundations; NATO and European Community.
- Consolidation and Expansion of European Community
- European Union.

12. Disintegration of Soviet Union and the Rise of the Unipolar World

- Factors leading to the collapse of Soviet Communism and Soviet Union, 1985-1991.
- Political Changes in East Europe 1989-2001.
- End of the Cold War and US Ascendancy in the World as the lone superpower.

Law

Paper-I

Constitutional and Administrative Law

- Constitution and Constitutionalism:The distinctive features of the Constitution.
- Fundamental Rights—Public interest litigation; Legal Aid; Legal services authority.
- Relationship between Fundamental rights, Directive principles and Fundamental duties.
- Constitutional Position of the President and relation with the Council of Ministers.
- Governor and his powers.
- **Supreme Court and the High Courts:**
  - Appointments and transfer.
  - Powers, functions and jurisdiction.
- **Centre, States and local bodies:**
  - Distribution of legislative powers between the Union and the States.
  - Local Bodies.
  - Administrative relationship among Union, State and Local Bodies.
  - Eminent domain-State property-common property-community property.
- Legislative powers, privileges and immunities.
- **Services under the Union and the States:**
  - Recruitment and conditions of services; Constitutional safeguards; Administrative tribunals.
  - Union Public Service Commission and StatePublic Service Commissions—Power andfunctions.
  - Election Commission—Power and functions.
- Emergency provisions.
- Amendment of the Constitution.
- Principle of Natural Justice—Emerging trends and judicial approach.
- Delegated legislation and its constitutionality.
- Separation of powers and constitutional governance.
- Judicial review of administrative action.
- Ombudsman: Lokayukta, Lokpal etc.

International Law

- Nature and Definition of International Law.
- Relationship between International Law and Municipal Law.
- State Recognition and State Succession.
- **Law of the sea:** Inland Waters,Territorial Sea, Contiguous Zone, Continental Shelf, Exclusive
- Economic Zone and High Seas.
- **Individuals**: Nationality, statelessness; Human Rights and procedures available for their enforcement.
- Territorial jurisdiction of States, Extradition and Asylum.
- **Treaties:** Formation, application, termination and reservation.
- **United Nations**: Its principal organs, powers and functions and reform.
- Peaceful settlement of disputes—different modes.
- Lawful recourse to force: aggressions, self-defence, intervention.
- Fundamental principles of international humanitarian law—International conventions and contemporary developments.
- Legality of the use of nuclear weapons; ban on testing of nuclear weapons; Nuclear non- proliferation treaty, CTST.
- International Terrorism, State sponsored terrorism, Hijacking, International Criminal Court.
- New International Economic Order and Monetary Law: WTO, TRIPS, GATT, IMF, World Bank.
- Protection and Improvement of the Human Environment: International Efforts.

Paper–II

Law of Crimes

- General principles of Criminal liability: mens rea and actus reus, mens rea in statutory offences
- Kinds of punishment and emerging trends as to abolition of capital punishment.
- Preparations and criminal attempt.
- General exceptions.
- Joint and constructive liability.
- Abetment.
- Criminal conspiracy.

- Offences against the State.
- Offences against public tranquility.
- Offences against human body.
- Offences against property.
- Offences against women.
- Defamation.
- Prevention of Corruption Act, 1988.
- Protection of Civil Rights Act, 1955 and subsequent legislative developments.
- Plea bargaining.

Law of Torts

- Nature and definition.
- Liability based upon fault and strict liability; Absolute liability.
- Vicarious liability including State Liability.
- General defences.
- Joint tort fessors.
- Remedies.
- Negligence.
- Defamation.
- Nuisance.
- Conspiracy.
- False imprisonment.
- Malicious prosecution.
- Consumer Protection Act, 1986.

Law of Contracts and Mercantile Law

- Nature and formation of contract/E-contract.
- Factors vitiating free consent.
- Void, voidable, illegal and unenforceable agreements.
- Performance and discharge of contracts.
- Quasi-contracts.
- Consequences of breach of contract.
- Contract of indemnity, guarantee and insurance.
- Contract of agency.

- Sale of goods and hire purchase.
- Formation and dissolution of partnership.
- Negotiable Instruments Act, 1881.
- Arbitration and Conciliation Act, 1996.
- Standard form contracts.

Contemporary Legal Developments

- Public Interest Litigation.
- Intellectual property rights—Concept, types/prospects.
- Information Technology Law including Cyber Laws—Concept, purpose/prospects.
- Competition Law—Concept, purpose/prospects.
- Alternate Dispute Resolution—Concept, types/prospects.
- Major statutes concerning environmental law.
- Right to Information Act.
- Trial by media.

Literature of the following languages

1. A candidate may be required to answer some or all the Questions in the language concerned.
2. In regard to the languages included in the Eighth Schedule to Constitution, the scripts will be the same as indicated in the table given relating to the Main Examination *(refer to page number 10)*.
3. Candidates should note that the questions not required to be answered in a specific language will have to be answered in the language medium indicated by them for answering papers on Essay, General Studies and Optional Subjects.
4. Answers must be written in the language chosen.

ASSAMESE

Paper–I

Section A: Language

- History of the origin and development of the Assamese Language —its position among the Indo-Aryan language—periods in its history.
- Development of Assamese prose.
- Vowels and consonants of the Assamese Language—Rules of phonetic changes with stress on Assamese coming down from Old Indo-Aryan.
- Assamese vocabulary—and its sources.
- Morphology of the language—conjugation—enclitic definitives and pleonastic suffixes.
- Dilectical divergences—the Standard colloquial and the Kamrupi dialect in particular.
- Assamese script—its evolution through the ages till 19th century A.D.

Section–B: Literary Criticism and Literary History

- Principles of literary criticism up to New criticism.
- Different literary genres.
- Development of literary forms in Assamese.
- Development of literary criticism in Assamese.
- Periods of the literary history of Assam from the earliest beginnings, i.e. from the period of the charyyageeta with their socio-cultural background: the proto Assamese Pre-Sankaradeva—Sankaradeva—Post-Sankaradeva—Modern period (from the coming of the Britishers)—Post-Independence period. Special emphasis is to be given on the Vaisnavite period, the gonaki and the post-independence periods.

Paper–II

This paper will require first-hand reading of the texts prescribed and will be designed to test the candidate's critical ability.

Section–A	
Râmâyana (Ayodhyâ Kânda	by Madhava Kandali only)
Pârijât-Harana	by Sankaradeva.
Râsakrîdâ	by Sankaradeva (From Kirtana Ghosa)
Bârgeet	by Madhavadeva.
Râjasûya	by Madhavadeva.
Kathâ-Bhâgavata(Books I and II)	by Baikurthanath
Section–B	
Mor Jeevan Soñwaran	by Lakshminath Bezbaroa.
Kripâbar Borbaruâr Kakatar Topola	by Lakshminath Bezbaroa.
Pratimâ	by Chandra KumarAgarwalla.
Gâonburhâ	by Padmanath GohainBarua.
Manomatî	by Rajanikanta Bordoloi.
Purani Asamîyâ Sâhitya	by Banikanta Kakati.
Kârengar Ligirî	by Jyotiprasad Agarwalla
Jeevanar Bâtat	by Bina Barva(BirinchiKumar Barua)
Mrityunjoy	by Birendrakumar Bhattacharyya
Samrât	by Navakanta Barua

BENGALI

Paper–I

History of Language and Literature

Section–A: Topics from the History of Bangla language

- The chronological track from Proto Indo-European to Bangla (Family tree with branches and approximate dates).
- Historical stages of Bangla (Old, Middle, New) and their linguistic features.
- Dialects of Bangla and their distinguishing characteristics.
- Elements of Bangla Vocabulary.
- Forms of Bangla Literary Prose—Sadhu and Chalit.
- Processes of language change relevant for Bangla:
- Apinihiti (Anaptyxis), Abhishruti (umlaut), Murdhanyibhavan (cerebralization), Nasikyibhavan (Nasalization), Samibhavan (Assimilation), Sadrishya (Analogy), Svaragama (Vowel insertion)—Adi Svaragama, Madhya Svaragama or Svarabhakti, Antya Svaragama, Svarasangati (Vowel harmony), y—shruti and w—shruti.
- Problems of standardization and reform of alphabet and spelling, and those of transliteration and Romanization.
- Phonology, Morphology and Syntax of Modern Bangla.
- (Sounds of Modern Bangla, Conjuncts; word formations, compounds; basic sentence patterns.)

Section–B: Topics from the History of Bangla Literature.

- Periodization of Bangla Literature: Old Bangla and Middle Bangla.
- Points of difference between modern and pre-modern Bangla Literature.
- Roots and reasons behind the emergence of modernity in Bangla Literature.
- Evolution of various Middle Bangla forms ; Mangal Kavyas, Vaishnava lyrics, Adapted narratives (Ramayana, Mahabharata, Bhagavata) and religious biographies.
- Secular forms in middle Bangla literature.
- Narrative and lyric trends in the nineteenth century Bangla poetry.
- Development of prose.

- Bangla dramatic literature (nineteenth century, Tagore, Post-1944 Bangla drama).
- Tagore and post-Tagoreans.
- Fiction, major authors:
- Bankimchandra, Tagore, Saratchandra, Bibhutibhusan, Tarasankar, Manik).
- Women and Bangla literature: creators and created.

Paper–II

Prescribed texts for close study

Section–A

- **Vaishnava Padavali** (Calcutta University)
- Poems of Vidyapati, Chandidas, Jnanadas, Govindadas and Balaramdas.
- **Chandimangal** Kalketu episode by Mukunda (Sahitya Akademi).
- **Chaitanya Charitamrita,** Madhya Lila by Krishnadas Kaviraj (Sahitya Akademi).
- **Meghnadbadh Kavya** by Madhusudan Dutta.
- **Kapalkundala** by Bankimchandra Chatterjee.
- **Samya** and **Bangadesher Krishak** by Bankimchandra Chatterjee.
- **Sonar Tari** by Rabindranath Tagore.
- **Chhinnapatravali** by Rabindranath Tagore.

Section–B

- **Raktakarabi** by Rabindranath Tagore.
- **Nabajatak** by Rabindranath Tagore.
- **Grihadaha** by Saratchandra Chatterjee.
- **Prabandha Samgraha,** Vol. 1, by Pramatha Choudhuri.
- **Aranyak** by Bibhutibhusan Banerjee.
- **Short stories** by Manik Bandyopadhyay: Atashi Mami, Pragaitihasik, Holud-Pora, Sarisrip, Haraner Natjamai, Chhoto-Bokulpurer Jatri, Kustharogir Bou, Jakey Ghush Ditey Hoy.
- **Shrestha Kavita** by Jibanananda Das.
- **Jagori** by Satinath Bhaduri.
- **Ebam Indrajit** by Badal Sircar.

Paper–I

History of Bodo Language and Literature

Section A: History of Bodo Language

- Homeland, language family, its present status and its mutual contact with Assamese.
  - Phonemes: Vowel and Consonant Phonemes.
  - Tones.
- Morphology: Gender, Case and Case endings, Plural suffix, Definitives, Verbal suffix.
- Vocabulary and its sources.
- Syntax: Types of sentences, Word Order.
- History of scripts used in writing Bodo Language since inception.

Section B: History of Bodo Literature

- General introduction of Bodo folk Literature.
- Contribution of the Missionaries.
- Periodization of Bodo Literature.
- Critical analysis of different genre (Poetry, Novel, Short Story and Drama).
- Translation Literature.

Paper–II

The paper will require first-hand reading of the texts prescribed and will be designed to test the critical ability of the candidates.

Section A

- Khonthai-Methai
  - (Edited by Madaram Brahma & Rupnath Brahma)
- Hathorkhi-Hala
- (Edited by Pramod Chandra Brahma)
- Boroni Gudi Sibsa Arw Aroz: Madaram Brahma
- Raja Nilambar: Dwarendra Nath Basumatary

- Bibar (prose section)
    - (Edited by Satish Chandra Basumatary).

Section B

- Bibi Bithai (Aida Nwi): Bihuram Boro
- Radab: Samar Brahma Chaudhury
- Okhrang Gongse Nangou: Brajendra Kumar Brahma
- Baisagu Arw Harimu: Laksheswar Brahma
- Gwdan Boro: Manoranjan Lahary
- Jujaini Or: Chittaranjan Muchahary
- Mwihoor: Dharanidhar Wary
- Hor Badi Khwmsi: Kamal Kumar Brahma
- Jaolia Dewan: Mangal Singh Hozowary
- Hagra Guduni Mwi: Nilkamal Brahma

DOGRI

Paper–I

History of Dogri Language And Literature

Section A: History of Dogri Language

- Dogri language: Origin and development through different stages.
- Linguistic boundaries of Dogri and its dialects.
- Characteristic features of Dogri Language.
- Structure of Dogri Langauge:
  - Sound Structure:
- Segmental: Vowels and Consonants
- Non-segmental: Length, Stress, Nasalization, Tone and Junture.
- Morphology of Dogri:
  - Inflection Categories: Gender, Number, Case, Person, Tense and Voice.
  - Word Formation; use of prefixes, infixes and suffixes.
  - Vocabulary: tatsam, tadbhav, foreign and regional.
- Sentence Structure; Major Sentence-types and their constituents, agreement and concord in Dogri syntax.
- Dogri Language and Scripts: Dogre/Dogra Akkhar, Devanagari and Persia.

Section B: History of Dogri Language

- A brief account of Pre-independence Dogri Literature: Poetry & Prose.
- Development of modern Dogri Poetry and main trends in Dogri Poetry.
- Development of Dogri short-story, main trends and prominent short-story writers.
- Development of Dogri Novel, main trends and contribution of Dogri Novelists.
- Development of Dogri Drama and contribution of prominent playwrights.
- Development of Dogri Prose; Essays, Memoirs and travelogues.
- An introduction to Dogri Folk Literature—Folk songs, Folk tales 7 Ballads.

Paper -II

Textual Criticism Of Dogri Literature

Section A: Poetry

- Azadi Paihle Di Dogri Kavita The following poets:

- Devi Ditta, Lakkhu, Ganga Ram, Ramdhan, Hardutt, Pahari Gandhi Baba Kanshi Ram & Permanand Almast
- Modern Dogri Poetry Azadi Bad Di Dogri Kavita The following poets:
- Kishan Smailpuri, Tara Smailpuri, Mohan Lal Sapolia, Yash Sharma, K.S. Madhukar, Padma Sachdev, Jitendra Udhampuri, Charan Singh and Prakash Premi
- Sheeraza Dogri Number 102, Ghazal Ank The following poets:
- Ram Lal Sharma, Ved Pal Deep, N.D. Jamwal, Shiv Ram Deep, Ashwini Magotra and Virendra Kesar
- Sheeraza Dogri Number 147, Ghazal Ank The following poets:
- R.N. Shastri, Jitendra Udhampuri, Champa Sharma and Darshan Darshi.
- Ramayan (Epic) by Shambhu Nath Sharma (up to Ayodhya Kand)
- Veer Gulab (Khand Kavya) by Dinoo Bhai Pant.

Section B: Prose

- Ajakani Dogri Kahani
  - The following Short Story Writers:
  - Madan Mohan Sharma, Narendra Khajuri and B.P. Sathe
- Ajakani Dogri Kahani Part-II
  - The following Short Story Writers:
  - Ved Rahi, Narsingh Dev Jamwal, Om Goswami, Chahttrapal, Lalit Magotra, Chaman Arora and Ratan Kesar.
- Khatha Kunj Bhag II
  - The following Story Writers:
  - Om Vidyarthi, Champa Sharma and Krishan Sharma.
- Meel Patthar (collection of short stories) by Bandhu Sharma.
- Kaiddi (Novel) by Desh Bandhu Dogra Nutan.
- Nanga Rukkh (Novel) by O.P. Sharma Sarathi.
- Nayaan (Drama) by Mohan Singh.
- Satrang (A collection of one act plays). The following play wrights:
- Vishwa Nath Khajuria, Ram Nath Shastri, Jitendra Sharma, Lalit Magotra and Madan Mohan Sharma.
- Dogri Lalit Nibandh The following authors:
- Vishwa Nath Khajuria, Narayan Mishra, Balkrishan Shastri, Shiv Nath, Shyam Lal Sharma, Lakshmi Narayan, D.C. Prashant, Ved Ghai, Kunwar Viyogi.

ENGLISH

The syllabus consists of two papers, designed to test a first-hand and critical reading of texts prescribed from the following periods in English Literature: Paper 1: 1600-1900 and Paper 2: 1900–1990.

There will be two compulsory questions in each paper: (a) A short-notes question related to the topics for general study, and (b) A critical analysis of UNSEEN passages both in prose and verse.

Paper–I

Texts for detailed study are listed below. Candidates will also be required to show adequate knowledge of the following topics and movements:

The Renaissance; Elizabethan and Jacobean Drama; Metaphysical Poetry; The Epic and the Mock-epic; Neo-classicism; Satire; The Romantic Movement; The Rise of the Novel; The Victorian Age.

Section A

- William Shakespeare: King Lear and The Tempest.
- John Donne. The following poems:
  - Canonization;
  - Death be not proud;
  - The Good Morrow;
  - On his Mistress going to bed;
  - The Relic;
- John Milton: Paradise Lost, I, II, IV, IX.
- Alexander Pope. The Rape of the Lock.
- William Wordsworth. The following poems:
  - Ode on Intimations of Immortality.
  - Tintern Abbey.
  - Three years she grew.
  - She dwelt among untrodden ways.
  - Michael.
  - Resolution and Independence.

- The World is too much with us.
- Milton, thou shouldst be living at this hour.
- Upon Westminster Bridge.

- Alfred Tennyson: In Memoriam.
- Henrik Ibsen: A Doll's House.

Section B

- Jonathan Swift, Gulliver's Travels.
- Jane Austen. Pride and Prejudice.
- Henry Fielding. Tom Jones.
- Charles Dickens. Hard Times.
- George Eliot. The Mill on the Floss.
- Thomas Hardy. Tess of the d Urbervilles.
- Mark Twain. The Adventures of Huckleberry Finn.

Paper–II

Texts for detailed study are listed below. Candidates will also be required to show adequate knowledge of the following topics and movements:

Modernism; Poets of the Thirties; The stream-of-consciousness Novel; Absurd Drama; Colonialism and Post-Colonialism; Indian Writing in English; Marxist, Psychoanalytical and Feminist approaches to literature; Post-Modernism.

Section A

- **William Butler Yeats. The following poems:**
  - Easter 1916.
  - The Second Coming.
  - A Prayer for my daughter.
  - Sailing to Byzantium.
  - The Tower.
  - Among School Children.
  - Leda and the Swan.
  - Meru.

- Lapis Lazuli.
- The Second Coming.
- Byzantium.

- **T.S. Eliot. The following poems:**
  - The Love Song of J. Alfred Prufrock.
  - Journey of the Magi.
  - Burnt Norton.
- **W.H. Auden. The following poems:**
  - Partition
  - Musee des Beaux Arts
  - In Memory of W.B. Yeats
  - Lay your sleeping head, my love
  - The Unknown Citizen
  - Consider
  - Mundus Et Infans
  - The Shield of Achilles
  - September 1, 1939
  - Petition
- John Osborne: Look Back in Anger.
- Samuel Beckett. Waiting for Godot.
- **Philip Larkin. The following poems:**
  - Next
  - Please
  - Deceptions
  - Afternoons
  - Days
  - Mr. Bleaney
- **A.K. Ramanujan. The following poems:**
  - Looking for a Cousin on a Swing
  - A River
  - Of Mothers, among other Things

- Love Poem for a Wife 1
- Small-Scale Reflections on a Great House
- Obituary

(All these poems are available in the anthology Ten Twentieth Century Indian Poets, edited by

R. Parthasarthy, published by Oxford University Press, New Delhi).

Section B

- Joseph Conrad. Lord Jim.
- James Joyce. Portrait of the Artist as a Young Man.
- D.H. Lawrence. Sons and Lovers.
- E.M. Forster. A Passage to India.
- Virginia Woolf. Mrs. Dalloway.
- Raja Rao. Kanthapura.
- V.S. Naipaul. A House for Mr. Biswas.

GUJARATI

Paper–I

Section A: Gujarati Language: Form and History

- History of Gujarati Language with special reference to New Indo-Aryan i.e. last one thousand years.
- Significant features of the Gujarati language: phonology, morphology and syntax.
- Major dialects: Surti, pattani, charotari and Saurashtri.

History of Gujarati Literature

Medieval:

- Jaina tradition
- Bhakti tradition: Sagun and Nirgun (Jnanmargi)
- Non-sectarian tradition (Laukik parampara)

Modern:

- Sudharak yug
- Pandit yug
- Gandhi yug
- Anu-Gandhi yug
- Adhunik yug

Section B

Literary Forms: (Salient features, history and development of the following literary forms:)

- **Medieval**
  - **Narratives:** Rasa, Akhyan and Padyavarta
  - **Lyrical:** Pada
- **Folk**
  - Bhavai
- **Modern**
  - **Fiction:** Novel and Short Story
  - Drama
  - Literary Essay
  - Lyrical Poetry

- **Criticism**
  - History of theoretical Gujarati criticism
  - Recent research in folk tradition.

Paper-II

The paper will require first-hand reading of the texts prescribed and will be designed to test the critical ability of the candidate.

Section A

- **Medieval**
  - Vasantvilas phagu—AJNATKRUT
  - Kadambari—BHALAN
  - Sudamacharitra—PREMANAND
  - Chandrachandravatini varta—SHAMAL
  - Akhegeeta—AKHO
- **Sudharakyug & Pandityug**
  - Mari Hakikat—NARMADASHA
  - Farbasveerah—DALPATRAM
  - Saraswatichandra-Part 1—GOVARDHANRAM TRIPATHI
  - Purvalap—'KANT' (MANISHANKAR RATNAJI BHATT)
  - Raino Parvat—RAMANBHAI NEELKANTH

Section B

- **Gandhiyug & Anu Gandhiyug**
  - Hind Swaraj—MOHANDAS KARAMCHAND GANDHI
  - Patanni Prabhuta—KANHAIYALAL MUNSHI
  - Kavyani Shakti—RAMNARAYAN VISHWANATH PATHAK
  - Saurashtrani Rasdhar-Part 1—ZAVERCHAND MEGHANI
  - Manvini Bhavai—PANNALAL PATEL
  - Dhvani—RAJENDRA SHAH
- **Adhunik yug**
  - Saptapadi—UMASHANKAR JOSHI
  - Janantike—SURESH JOSHI
  - Ashwatthama—SITANSHU YASHASCHANDRA.

HINDI

Paper–I

Section A: History of Hindi Language and Nagari Lipi

- Grammatical and applied forms of Apbhransh, Awahatta & Arambhik Hindi.
- Development of Braj and Awadhi as Literary language during medieval period.
- Early form of Khari-boli in Siddha-Nath Sahitya, Khusero, Sant Sahitaya, Rahim etc. and Dakhni Hindi.
- Development of Khari-boli and Nagari Lipi during 19th Century.
- Standardisation of Hindi Bhasha & Nagari Lipi.
- Development of Hindi as a National Language during freedom movement.
- The development of Hindi as a National Language of Union of India.
- Scientific & Technical Development of Hindi Language.
- Prominent dialects of Hindi and their inter-relationship.
- Salient features of Nagari Lipi and the efforts for its reform & Standard form of Hindi.
- Grammatical structure of Standard Hindi.

Section B: History of Hindi Literature

- The relevance and importance of Hindi literature and tradition of writing History of Hindi Literature.
- Literary trends of the following four periods of history of Hindi Literature.
  - **A:** Adikal—Sidh, Nath and Raso Sahitya.
  - Prominent poets—Chandvardai, Khusaro, Hemchandra, Vidyapati.
  - **B:** Bhaktikal—Sant Kavyadhara, Sufi Kavyadhara, Krishna Bhaktidhara and Ram Bhaktidhara.
  - Prominent Poets—Kabir, Jayasi, Sur & Tulsi.
  - **C:** Ritikal—Ritikavya, Ritibaddhkavya & Riti Mukta Kavya. Prominent Poets—Keshav, Bihari, Padmakar and Ghananand.
  - **D:** Adhunik Kal—
  - Renaissance, the development of Prose, Bharatendu Mandal.
  - Prominent Writers—Bharatendu, Bal Krishna Bhatt & Pratap Narain Mishra.
  - Prominent trends of modern Hindi Poetry: Chhayavad, Pragativad, Prayogvad, Nai Kavita, Navgeet and Contemporary poetry and Janvadi Kavita.

- Prominent Poets—Maithili Sharan Gupta, Prasad, Nirala, Mahadevi, Dinkar, Agyeya, Muktibodh, Nagarjun.

Katha Sahitya

- Upanyas & Realism
- The origin and development of Hindi Novels.
- ProminentNovelists—Premchand, Jain-endra, Yashpal, Renu and Bhism Sahani.
- The origin and development of Hindi short story.
- Prominent Short Story Writers—Premchand, Prasad, Agyeya, Mohan Rakesh & Krishna Sobti.

Drama & Theatre

- The Origin & Development of Hindi Drama.
- Prominent Dramatists—Bharatendu, Prasad, Jagdish Chandra Mathur, Ram Kumar Verma, Mohan Rakesh.
- The development of Hindi Theatre.

Criticism

- The origin and development of Hindi criticism: Saiddhantik, Vyavharik, Pragativadi, Manovishleshanvadi & Nai Alochana.
- Prominent critics—Ramchandra Shukla, Hajari Prasad Dwivedi, Ram Vilas Sharma & Nagendra.

The other form of Hindi prose—Lalit Nibandh,Rekhachitra, Sansmaran, Yatra-vrittant.

Paper–II

The paper will require first-hand reading of the prescribed texts and will test the critical ability of the candidates.

Section A

- **Kabir:** Kabir Granthawali, Ed. Shyam Sundar Das (First hundred Sakhis)
- **Soordas:** Bhramar Geetsar, Ed. Ramchandra Shukla (First hundred Padas)
- **Tulsidas:** Ramcharit Manas (Sundar Kand) Kavitawali (Uttarkand)
- **Jayasi:** Padmawat Ed. Shyam Sundar Das (Sinhal Dwip Khand & Nagmativiyog Khand)

- **Bihari:** Bihari Ratnakar Ed. Jagnnath Prasad Ratnakar (First 100 Dohas)
- **Maithili Sharan Gupta:** Bharat Bharati
- **Prasad:** Kamayani (Chinta and Shraddha Sarg)
- **Nirala:** Rag-Virag, Ed. Ram Vilas Sharma (Ram Ki Shakti Pooja & Kukurmutta)
- **Dinkar:** Kurukshetra
- **Agyeya:** Angan Ke Par Dwar (Asadhya Veena)
- **Muktiboth:** Brahm Rakhashas
- **Nagarjun:** Badal Ko Ghirte Dekha Hai, Akal Ke Bad, Harijan Gatha.

Section B

- **Bharatendu:** Bharat Durdasha
- **Mohan Rakesh:** Ashadh Ka Ek Din
- **Ramchandra:** Chintamani (Part I) (KavitaKya Shukla Hai, ShraddhaAurBhakti)
- **Dr. Satyendra:** Nibandh Nilaya—Bal Krishna Bhatt, Premchand, Gulab Rai, Hajari Prasad Dwivedi, Ram Vilas Sharma, Agyeya, Kuber Nath Rai.
- Premchand Godan, Premchand ki Sarvashreshtha Kahaniyan, Ed. Amrit Rai/ Manjusha—Prem Chand ki Sarvashreshtha Kahaniyan. Ed. Amrit Rai.
- **Prasad:** Skandgupta
- **Yashpal:** Divya
- **Phaniswar Nath:** Maila Anchal Renu
- **Mannu Bhandari:** Mahabhoj
- **Rajendra Yadav:** Ek Dunia Samanantar (All Stories)

Kannada

Paper-I

Section A: History of Kannada Language

- What is Language ? General characteristics of Language. Dravidian Family of Languages and its specific features. Antiquity of Kannada Language. Different phases of its Development.
- Dialects of Kannada Language: Regional and Social. Various aspects of developments of Kannada Language: phonological and Semantic changes. Language borrowing.

History of Kannada Literature

Ancient Kannada literature: Influence and Trends, Poets for study: Specified poets from Pampa to Ratnakara Varni are to be studied in the light of contents, form and expression: Pampa, Janna, Nagachandra.

- **Medieval Kannada literature:** Influence and Trends.
- **Vachana Literature:** Basavanna, Akka Mahadevi.
- **Medieval Poets:** Harihara, Raghavanka, Kumara-Vyasa.
- **Dasa literature:** Purandara and Kanaka.
- **Sangataya:** Ratnakarvarni
- Modern Kannada literature: Influence, trends and ideologies, Navodaya, Pragatishila, Navya, Dalita and Bandaya.

Section B: Poetics and Literary Criticism

- Definition and concepts of poetry; Word, Meaning, Alankara, Reeti, Rasa, Dhwani, Auchitya.
- Interpretations of Rasa Sutra.
- Modern Trends of literary criticism: Formalist, Historical, Marxist, Feminist, Post-colonial criticism.

Cultural History of Karnataka

- Contribution of Dynasties to the culture of Karnataka: Chalukyas of Badami and Kalyani, Rashtrakutas, Hoysalas, Vijayanagara rulers, in literary context.
- Major religions of Karnataka and their cultural contribution.
- Arts of Karnataka ; Sculpture, Architecture, Painting, Music, Dance in the literary context.

- Unification of Karnataka and its impact of Kannada literature.

Paper-II

The Paper will require first-hand reading of the Texts prescribed and will be designed to test the critical ability of the candidates.

Section A: Old Kannada Literature

- Vikramaarjuna Vijaya of Pampa (Cantos 12 & 13), (Mysore University Pub.)
- Vaddaraadhane (Sukumaraswamyia Kathe, Vidyutchorana Kathe)

Medieval Kannada Literature

- Vachana, Kammata, Ed. K. Marulasiddappa K.R. Nagaraj (Bangalore University Pub.)
- Janapriya Kanakasamputa, Ed. D. Javare Gowda (Kannada and Culture Directorate, Bangalore)
- Nambiyannana Ragale, Ed., T.N. Sreekantaiah (Ta. Vem. Smaraka Grantha Male, Mysore)
- Kumaravyasa Bharata: Karna Parva (Mysore University)
- Bharatesha Vaibhava Sangraha Ed Ta. Su. Shama Rao (Mysore University)

Section B: Modern Kannada Literature

- **Poetry:** Hosagannada Kavite, Ed. G.H. Nayak (Kannada Saahitya Parishattu, Bangalore)
- **Novel:** Bettada Jeeva—Shivarama Karanta Madhavi—Anupama Niranjana Odalaala-Deva-nuru Mahadeva
- **Short Story:** Kannada Sanna Kathegalu, Ed. G.H. Nayak (Sahitya Academy, New Delhi)
- **Drama:** Shudra Tapaswi—Kuvempu. Tughalak—Girish Karnad.
- **Vichara Sahitya:** Devaru—A.N. Moorty Rao (Pub: D.V.K.Moorty, Mysore.)

Folk Literature

- Janapada Swaroopa—Dr. H.M. Nayak. (Ta. Vem. Smaraka Grantha Male, Mysore.)
- Janpada Geetaanjali—Ed. D. Javare Gowda.(Pub: Sahitya Academy, New Delhi).
- Kannada Janapada Kathegalu—Ed. J.S. Paramashiviaah (Mysore University).
- Beedi Makkalu Beledo. Ed. Kalegowda Nagavara (Pub: Bangalore University).
- Savirada Ogatugalu—Ed. S.G. Imrapura.

KASHMIRI

Paper-I

Section A

- Genealogical relationship of the Kashmiri language: various theories.
- Areas of occurence and dialects (geographical/social)
- Phonology and grammar:
  - Vowel and consonant system;
  - Nouns and pronouns with various case inflections;
  - Verbs: various types and tenses.
- Syntactic structure:
  - Simple, active and declarative statements;
  - Coordination;
  - Relativisation.

Section B

- Kashmiri literature in the 14th century (Socio-cultural and intellectual background with special reference to *Lal Dyad* and *Sheikhul Alam).*
- Nineteenth century Kashmiri literature (development of various genres: *vatsun; ghazal and* mathnavi.
- Kashmiri literature in the first half of the twentieth century (with special reference to Mahjoor and Azad; various literary influences).
- Modern Kashmiri literature (with special reference to the development of the short story, drama, novel and nazm).

Paper-II

Section A

- Intensive study of Kashmiri poetry up to the nineteenth century:
  - Lal Dyad,
  - Sheikhul Aalam
  - Habba Khatoon
- **Kashmiri poetry:** 19th Century
  - Mahmood Gami *(Vatsans)*

- Maqbool Shah *(Gulrez)*
- Rasool Mir *(Ghazals)*
- Abdul Ahad Nadim *(N'at)*
- Krishanjoo Razdan *(Shiv Lagun)*
- Sufi Poets (Test in *Sanglaab*, published by the Deptt. of Kashmiri, University of Kashmir)

- Twentieth Century Kashmiri poetry (text in *Azich Kashir Shairi,* published by the Deptt. of Kashmiri, University of Kashmir).
- Literary criticism and research work: development and various trends.

Section B

- An analytical study of the short story in Kashmiri.
    - *Afsana Majmu'a,* published by the Deptt. of Kashmiri, University of Kashmir.
    - *Kashur Afsana Az,* published by the Sahitya Akademi.
    - *Hamasar Kashur Afsana,* published by the Sahitya Akademi.

The following short story writers only: Akhtar Mohi-ud Din, Kamil, Hari Krishan Kaul, Hraday Kaul Bharti, Bansi Nirdosh, Gulshan Majid.

- **Novel in Kashmiri:**
    - *Mujrim by* G. N. Gowhar
    - *Marun*—Ivan Ilyichun, (Kashmiri version of Tolstoy's) The Death of Ivan Ilyich (published by Kashmiri Deptt.)

Drama in Kashmiri

- *Natuk Kariv Band by* Hari Krishan Kaul
- Qk Angy Natuk, ed. Motilal Keemu, published by the Sahitya Akademi.
- *Razi Oedipus,* tr. Naji Munawar, published by the Sahitya Akademi.
- Kashmiri Folk Literature:
    - *Kashur Luki Theatre* by Mohammad Subhan Bhagat,published by the Deptt. of Kashmiri, University of Kashmir.
    - *Kashiry Luki Beeth* (all volumes) published by the J&K Cultural Akademy.

KONKANI

Paper -I

Section A: History of the Konkani Language

- Origin and development of the language and influences on it.
- Major variants of Konkani and their linguistic features.
- Grammatical and lexicographic work in Konkani, including a study of cases, adverbs, indeclinables and voices.
- Old Standard Konkani, New Standard and Standardisation problems.

Section B: History of Konkani Literature

Candidates would be expected to be well-acquainted with Konkani literature and its social and cultural background and consider the problems and issues arising out of them.

- History of Konkani literature from its probable source to the present times, with emphasis on its major works, writers and movements.
- Social and cultural background of the making of Konkani literature from time to time.
- Indian and Western influences on Konkani literature, from the earliest to modern times.
- Modern literary trends in the various genres and regions including a study of Konkani folklore.

Paper-II

Textual Criticism of Konkani Literature

The paper will be designed to test the candidate's critical and analytical abilities. Candidates would be expected to be well-acquainted with Konkani Literature and required to have first-hand reading of the following texts:

Section A: Prose

- Konkani Mansagangotri (excluding poetry) ed. by Prof: Olivinho Gomes.
- Old Konkani language and literature—the Portuguese Role
- Otmo Denvcharak—a novel by A. V. da Cruz.

  - Vadoll ani Varem—a novel by Antonio Pereira.
  - Devache Kurpen—a novel by V.J.P. Saldanha.
- Vajralikhani—Shenoy goem-bab-An anthology-ed. by Shantaram Varde Valavalikar.
  - Konkani Lalit Niband—Essays-ed. by Shyam Verenkar.
  - Teen Dasakam—An anthology—ed. by Chandrakant Keni.
- Demand—Drama-by Pundalik Naik.
  - Kadambini: A Miscellany of Modern Prose—ed. by Prof. O.J.F. Gomes and Smt. P.S. Tadkodkar.
  - Ratha Tujeo Ghudieo—by Smt. Jayanti Naik.

Section B: Poetry

- Ev ani Mori: Poetry by Eduardo Bruno de Souza.
- Abravanchem Yadnyadan—by Luis Mascarenhas.
- Godde Ramayan—ed. by R.K. Rao.
- Ratnahar I and II—collection of poems—ed. R. V. Pandit.
- Zayo Zuyo—poems- Manohar L. Sardessai.
- Kanadi Mati Konkani Kavi—Anthology ofPoems—ed. Pratap Naik.
- Adrushatache Kalle—Poems by Pandurang Bhangui.
- Yaman—Poems by Madhav Borkar.

MAITHILI

Paper–I

History of Maithili Language and its Literature

Part A: History of Maithili Language

- Place of Maithili in Indo-European Language family.
- Origin and development of Maithili language. (Sanskrit, Prakrit, Avhatt, Maithili)
- Periodic division of Maithili Language. (Beginning, Middle era, Modern era).
- Maithili and its different dialects.
- Relationship between Maithili and other Eastern languages (Bengali, Asamese, Oriya)
- Origin and Development of Tirhuta Script.
- Pronouns and Verbs in Maithili Language.

Part B: History of Maithili Literature

- Background of Maithili Literature (Religious, Economic, Social, Cultural).
- Periodic division of Maithili literature.
- Pre-Vidyapati Literature.
- Vidyapati and his tradition.
- Medieval Maithili Drama (Kirtaniya Natak, Ankia Nat, Maithili dramas written in Nepal).
- Maithili Folk Literature (Folk Tales, Folk Drama, Folk Stories, Folk Songs).
- Development of different literary forms in modern era:
    - Prabandh-kavya
    - Muktak-kavya
    - Novel
    - Short Story
    - Drama
    - Essay
    - Criticism
    - Memoirs
    - Translation
- Development of Maithili Magazines and Journals.

Paper -II

The paper will require first-hand reading of the prescribed texts and will test the critical ability of the candidates.

Part–A

- Vidyapati Geet-Shati—Publisher: Sahitya Akademi, New Delhi (Lyrics— 1 to 50)
- Govind Das Bhajanavali—Publisher: Maithili Acadamy, Patna (Lyrics— 1 to 25)
- Krishnajanm—Manbodh
- Mithilabhasha Ramayana—Chanda Jha (only Sunder-Kand)
- Rameshwar Charit Mithila Ramayan—Lal Das (only Bal-kand)
- Keechak-Vadh—Tantra Nath Jha.
- Datta-Vati—Surendra Jah 'Suman' (only 1st and 2nd Cantos).
- Chitra-Yatri
- Samakaleen Maithili Kavita—Publisher: Sahitaya Akademi, New Delhi.

Part-B

- Varna Ratnakar—Jyotirishwar (only 2nd Kallol)
- Khattar Kakak Tarang—Hari Mohan Jha
- Lorik—Vijaya Manipadma
- Prithvi Putra—Lalit
- Bhaphait Chahak Jinagi—Sudhanshu 'Shekhar' Choudhary
- Kriti Rajkamlak—Publisher: Maithili Acadamy, Patna (First Ten Stories only)
- Katha–Sangrah–Publisher: Maithili Acadamy, Patna.

MALAYALAM

Paper-I

Section A

1. Early phase of Malayalam Language:

- 1.1 Various theories: Origin from proto Dravidian, Tamil, Sanskrit.
- 1.2 Relation between Tamil and Malayalam: Six nayas of A. R. Rajarajavarma.
- 1.3 Pattu School—Definition, Ramacharitam, later pattu works—Niranam Krishnagatha. works and

2. Linguistic features of

Manipravalam definition. Language of early manipravala works—Champu, Sandesakavya, Chandrotsava, minor works. Later manipravala works—medieval Champu and Attakkatha.

Folklore—Southern and Northern ballads, Mappila songs.

Early Malayalam Prose— Bhashakautaliyam, Brahmandapuranam, Attaprakaram, Kramadipika and Nambiantamil.

3. Standardisation of Malayalam

- Peculiarities of the language of Pana, Kilippattu and Tullal.
- Contributions of indigenous and European missionaries to Malayalam.
- Characteristics of contemporary Malayalam; Malayalam as administrative language.

Language of scientific and technical literature—media language.

Section B: Literary History

4. Ancient and Medieval Literature

- Pattu—Ramacharitam, Niranam Works and Krishnagatha.
- Manipravalam—early and medieval manipravala works including attakkatha and champu.
- Folk Literature.
- Kilippattu, Tullal and Mahakavya.

5. Modern Literature—Poetry

- Venmani poets and contemporaries.
- The advent of Romanticism—Poetry of Kavitraya i.e., Asan, Ulloor and Vallathol.
- Poetry after Kavitraya.
- Modernism in Malayalam Poetry.

6. Modern Literature—Prose

- Drama.
- Novel.
- Short story.
- Biography, travelogue, essay and criticism.

Paper-II

This paper will require first hand reading of the texts prescribed and is designed to test the candidate's critical ability.

Section A

Unit 1

- Ramacharitam—Patalam 1.
- Kannassaramayanam—Balakandam first 25 stanzas.
- Unnunilisandesam—Purvabhagam 25 slokas including Prastavana.
- Mahabharatham Kilippattu—Bhishmaparvam.

Unit 2

- Kumaran Asan—Chintavisthayaya Sita.
- Vailoppilli—Kutiyozhikkal.
- G. Sankara Kurup—Perunthachan.
- N. V. Krishna Variar—Tivandiyile pattu.

Unit 3

- O. N. V.—Bhumikkoru Charamagitam.
- Ayyappa Panicker—Kurukshetram.
- Akkittam—Pandatha Messanthi.
- Attur Ravivarma—Megharupan.

Unit 4

- O. Chanthu Menon—Indulekha.
- Thakazhy—Chemmin.

Section B

O. V. Vijayan—Khasakkinte Ithihasam.

Unit 5

- M. T. Vasudevan Nair—Vanaprastham (Collection).
- N. S. Madhavan—Higvitta (Collection).
- C. J. Thomas—1128-il Crime 27.

Unit 6

- Kuttikrishna Marar—Bharataparyatanam.
- M. K. Sanu—Nakshatrangalute Snehabhajanam.
- V. T. Bhatttathirippad—Kannirum Kinavum.

MANIPURI

Paper-I

Section A: Language

- General characteristics of Manipuri Language and history of its development; its importance and status among the Tibeto-Burman Languages of North-East India; recent development in the study of Manipuri Language; evolution and study of old Manipuri script.
- **Significant features of Manipuri Language:**
  - Phonology: Phoneme-vowels, consonants juncture, tone, consonant cluster and its occurrence, syllable-its structure, pattern and types.
  - Morphology: Word-class, root and its types; affix and its types; grammatical categories-gender, number, person, case, tense and aspects, process of compounding (samas and sandhi).
  - Syntax: Word order; types of sentences, phrase and clause structures.

Section B

- **Literary History of Manipuri:**
  - Early period (up to 17th Century)–Social and cultural background; Themes, diction and style of the works.
  - Medieval period (18th and 19th Century)-Social, religious and political background; Themes, diction and style of the works.
  - Modern period-Growth of major literary forms; change of Themes, diction and style.
- **Manipuri Folk Literature:** Legend, Folktale, Folksong, Ballad, Proverb and Riddle.
- **Aspects of Manipuri Culture:**
  - Pre-Hindu Manipuri Faith; Advent of Hinduism and the process of syncreticism; Performing arts-Lai Haraoba, Maha Ras;
  - Indegenous games-Sagol Kangjei, Khong Kangjei, Kang.

Paper-II

This paper will require first hand reading of the texts prescribed and will be designed to test candidate's critical ability to assess them.

Section A: Old and Medieval Manipuri Literature:

- **Old Manipuri Literature:**

- **O. Bhogeswar Singh (Ed.):** Numit Kappa
- **M. Gourachandra Singh (Ed.):** Thawanthaba Hiran
- **N. Khelchandra Singh (Ed.):** Naothingkhong
- Phambal Kaba
- **M. Chandra Singh (Ed.):** Panthoibi Khonggul

- **Medieval Manipuri Literature:**
  - **M. Chandra Singh (Ed.):** Samsok Ngamba
  - **R.K. Snahal Singh (Ed.):** Ramayana Adi Kanda
  - **N. Khelchandra Singh (Ed.):** Dhananjoy Laibu Ningba
  - **O. Bhogeswar Singh (Ed.):** Chandrakirti Jila Changba

Section B

Modern Manipuri Literature:

(a) Poetry and Epic

Poetry

- Manipuri Sheireng (Pub) Manipuri Sahitya Parishad, 1998 (Ed.)
- **Kh. Chaoba Singh:** Pi Thadoi, Lamgi Chekla Amada, Loktak
  - **Dr. L. Kamal Singh:** Nirjanata, Nirab Rajani
  - **A. Minaketan Singh:** Kamalda, Nonggumlalkkhoda.
  - **L. Samarendra Singh:** Ingagi Nong, Mamang Leikai Thambal Satle
  - **E. Nilakanta Singh:** Manipur, Lamangnaba
  - **Shri Biren:** Tangkhul Hui
  - **Th. Ibopishak:** Anouba Thunglaba Jiba.
- Kanchi Sheireng. (Pub) Manipur University 1998 (Ed.)
- **Dr. L. Kamal Singh:** Biswa-Prem
  - **Shri Biren:** Chaphadraba Laigi Yen Th. Ibopishak: Norok Patal Prithivi

Epic

- **A. Dorendrajit Singh:** Kansa Bodha
- **H. Anganghal Singh:** Khamba-Thoibi Sheireng(San-Senba, Lei Langba,Shamu Khonggi Bichar)

Drama:

- **S. Lalit Singh:** Areppa Marup

- **G.C. Tongbra:** Matric Pass
- **A. Samarendra:** Judge Saheb ki Imung

(b) Novel, Short-story and Prose:

Novel

- **Dr. L. Kamal Singh:** Madhabi
- **H. Anganghal Singh:** Jahera
- **H. Guno Singh:** Laman
- **Pacha Meetei:** Imphal Amasung, Magilshing, Nungsitki Phibam

Short-story

- Kanchi Warimacha (Pub) Manipur University 1997(Ed.)
- **R.K. Shitaljit Singh:** Kamala Kamala
- **M.K. Binodini:** Eigi Thahoudraba Heitup Lalu
- **Kh. Prakash:** Wanom Shareng
- Parishadki Khangatlaba Warimacha (Pub) Manipuri Sahitya Parishad 1994 (Ed.)
  - **S. Nilbir Shastri:** Loukhatpa
  - **R.K. Elangba:** Karinunggi
- Anouba Manipuri Warimacha (Pub) The Cultural Forum Manipur 1992 (Ed.)
  - **N. Kunjamohon Singh:** Ijat Tanba
  - **E. Dinamani:** Nongthak Khongnang

Prose

- Warenggi Saklon [Due Part] (Pub) The Cultural Forum Manipur 1992 (Ed.)
- **Kh. Chaoba Singh:** Khamba-Thoibigi WariAmasung Mahakavya
- Kanchi Wareng (Pub) Manipur University, 1998 (Ed.)
- **B. Manisana Shastri:** Phajaba
- **Ch. Manihar Singh:** Lai-Haraoba
- Apunba Wareng (Pub) Manipur University, 1986 (Ed.)
- **Ch. Pishak Singh:** Samaj Amasung Sanskriti
- **M.K. Binodini:** Thoibidu Warouhouida
- **Eric Newton:** Kalagi Mahousa (translated by I.R. Babu)
- Manipuri Wareng (Pub) The Cultural Forum Manipur 1999 (Ed.)
- **S. Krishnamohan Singh:** Lan

MARATHI

Paper-I

Language and Folk-lore

Section A

Nature and Functions of Language (with reference to Marathi)

- Language as a signifying system: Langue and Parole; Basic functions; Poetic Language; Standard Language and dialect; Language variations according to social parameters.
- Linguistic features of Marathi in thirteenth century and seventeenth century.
- Dialects of Marathi Ahirani; Varhadi; Dangi.
- Marathi Grammar
- Parts of Speech; Case-system; Prayog-vichar (Voice).
- Nature and kinds of Folk-lore (with special reference to Marathi)
- Lok-Geet, Lok Katha, Lok Natya.

Section B: History of Literature and Literary Criticism

History of Marathi Literature

- From beginning to 1818 AD, with special reference to the following: The Mahanubhava writers, the Varkari poets, the Pandit poets, the Shahirs, Bakhar Literature.
- From 1850 to 1990, with special reference to developments in the following major forms: Poetry, Fiction (Novel and Short Story), Drama; and major literary currents and movements, Romantic, Realist, Modernist, Dalit, Gramin, Feminist.
- Literary Criticism
  - Nature and function of Literature;
  - Evaluation of Literature;
  - Nature, Objectives and Methods of Criticism;
  - Literature, Culture and Society.

Paper-II

Textual study of prescribed literary works.

The paper will require first-hand reading of the texts prescribed and will be designed to test the candidate's critical ability.

- 'Smritisthala'
- Mahatma Jotiba Phule
  - ''Shetkaryacha Asud' 'Sarvajanik Satyadharma'
- **S.V. Ketkar**
  - 'Brahmankanya'
- **P.K. Atre**
  - 'Sashtang Namaskar'
- Sharchchandra Muktibodh 'Jana Hey Volatu Jethe'
- Uddhav Shelke 'Shilan'
- **Baburao Bagul**
  - 'Jevha Mi Jaat Chorli Hoti'
- **Gouri Deshpande**
  - 'Ekek Paan Galavaya'
- **P.I. Sonkamble**
  - 'Athavaṅinche Pakshi'
- 'Namadevanchi Abhangawani' Ed: Inamdar, Relekar, Mirajkar Modern Book Depot, Pune
- **'Painjan'**
  - Ed: M.N. Adwant
  - Sahitya Prasar Kendra, Nagpur
- **'Damayanti-Swayamvar'**
  - By Raghunath Pandit
- **'Balakvinchi Kavita'**
  - By Balkavi
- **'Vishakha'**
  - By Kusumagraj
- 'Maridgandh'

Section A: Prose

- 'Smritisthala'
- **Mahatma Jotiba Phule**
  - ''Shetkaryacha Asud'
  - 'Sarvajanik Satyadharma'
- **S.V. Ketkar**
  - 'Brahmankanya'

- **P.K. Atre**
  - 'Sashtang Namaskar'
- Sharchchandra Muktibodh
  - 'Jana Hey Volalu Jethe'
- **Uddhav Shelke**
  - 'Shilan'
- **Baburao Bagul**
  - 'Jevha Mi Jaat Chorli Hoti'
- Gouri Deshpande
  - 'Ekek Paan Galavaya'
- P.I. Sonkamble
  - 'Athavaninche Pakshi'

Section B: Poetry

- 'Namadevanchi Abhangawani'
  - Ed: Inamdar, Relekar, Mirajkar
  - Modern Book Depot, Pune
- **'Painjan'**
  - Ed : M.N. Adwant
  - Sahitya Prasar Kendra, Nagpur
- **'Damayanti-Swayamvar'**
  - By Raghunath Pandit
- **'Balakvinchi Kavita'**
  - By Balkavi
- **'Vishakha'**
  - By Kusumagraj
- **'Maridgandh'**
  - By Vinda Karandikar
- **'Jahirnama'**
  - By Narayan Surve
- **'Sandhyakalchya Kavita'**
  - By Grace
- **'Ya Sattet Jeev Ramat Nahi'**
  - By Namdev Dhasal

NEPALI

Paper-I

Section A

History of the origin and development of Nepali as one of the new Indo Aryan Languages. Fundamentals of Nepali Grammar and phonology:

- Nominal forms and categories:—
  - Gender, Number, Case, Adjectives, Pronouns, Avyayas
- Verbal forms and categories:
  - Tense, Aspects, Voice, Roots and Fixes
- Nepali Swara and Vyanjana;
  - Major Dialects of Nepali
  - Standardisation and Modernisation of Nepali with special reference to language movements (viz. Halanta Bahiskar, Jharrovad etc.)
  - Teaching of Nepali language in India—Its history and development with special reference to its socio-cultural aspects.

Section B

- History of Nepali literature with special reference to its development in India.
- Fundamental concepts and theories of Literature: Kavya/Sahitya, Kavya Prayojan, Literary genres, Shabda Shakti, Rasa, Alankara, Tragedy, Comedy, Aesthetics, Stylistics.
- Major literary trends and movements: Swachchhandatavad, Yatharthavad, Astitwavad, Ayamik Movement Contemporary Nepali writings, Postmodernism.
- Nepali folklores (the following folk-form only)—Sawai, Jhyaurey, Selo, Sangini, Lahari.

Paper-II

This paper will require first hand reading of the texts prescribed below and questions will be designed to test the candidate's critical acumen.

Section–A	
Santa Jnandil Das	Udaya Lahari
Lekhnath Poudyal	Tarun Tapasi (Vishrams III, V, VI, XII, XV, XVIII only)
Agam Sing Giri	Jaleko Pratibimba Royeko Pratidhwani (The following Poems only-Prasawako Chichyahatsanga Byunjheko Ek Raat, Chhorolai, Jaleko Pratibimba: Royeko Pratidhwani, Hamro Akashmani Pani Hunchha Ujyalo, Tihar).
Haribhakta Katuwal	Yo Zinadagi Khai Ke Zindagi: (The following poems only-Jeevan: Ek Dristi, Yo Zindagi Khai Ke Zindagi, Akashka Tara Ke Tara, Hamilai Nirdho Nasamjha, Khai Manyata Yahan Atmahutiko Balidan Ko).
Balkrishna Sama	Prahlad.
Manbahadur Mukhia	Andhyaroma Banchneharu (The following One-Act only-Andhyaroma Banchneharu' 'Suskera')
Section–B	
Indra Sundas	Sahara.
Lilbahadur Chhetri	Brahmaputra ko Chheuchhau
Rupnarayan Sinha	Katha Navaratna (The following stories only—Biteka Kura, Jimmewari Kasko, Dhanamatiko Cinema—Swapna, Vidhwasta Jeevan).
Indrabahadur Rai	Vipana Katipaya (The following stories only—Raatbhari Huri Chalyo, Jayamaya Aphumatra Lekhapani Aipugi, Bhagi, Ghosh Babu, Chhutuaiyo).
Sanu Lama	**Katha Sampaad** (The following stories only—Swasni Manchhey, Khani Tarma Ekdin, Phurbale Gaun Chhadyo, Asinapo Manchhey).
Laxmi Prasad	**Laxmi Nibandha** Devkota **Sangraha** (The following essays only—Sri Ganeshaya Namha, Nepali Sahityako Itihasma Sarvashrestha Purus, Kalpana, Kala Ra Jeevan, Gadha Buddhiman ki Guru?)
Ramkrishna Sharma	**Das Gorkha** (The following essays only—Kavi, Samaj Ra Sahitya, Sahityama Sapekshata, Sahityik Ruchiko Praudhata, Nepali Sahityako Pragati).

ODIA

Paper-I

Section A: History of Odia Language

- Origin and development of Odia Language—Influence of Austric, Dravidian, Perso— Arabic and English on Odia Language.
- Phonetics and Phonemics: Vowels, Consonants Principles of changes in Odia sounds.
- Morphology: Morphemes (free, bound compound and complex), derivational and inflectional affixes, case inflection, conjugation of verb.
- Syntax: Kinds of sentences and their trans-formation, structure of sentences.
- Semantics—Different types of change in meaning. Euphemism.
- Common errors in spellings, grammatical uses and construction of sentences.
- Regional variations in Odia Language (Western, Southern and Northern Odia) and Dialects (Bhatri and Desia).

Section B: History of Odia Literature

- Historical backgrounds (social, cultural and political) of Odia Literature of different periods.
- Ancient epics, ornate kavyas and padavalis.
- Typical structural forms of Odia Literature (Koili, Chautisa, Poi, Chaupadi, Champu).
- Modern trends in poetry, drama short story, novel essay and literary criticism.

Paper-II

Critical Study of texts: The paper will require first hand reading of the text and test the critical ability of the candidate.

Section A: Poetry (Ancient)

- Sãralã Dãs–Shanti Parva from Mahãbhãrata.
- Jaganãth Dãs–Bhãgabata, XI Skadhã–Jadu Avadhuta Sambãda.
- (Medieval)
- Dinakrushna Dãs–Raskallola–(Chhãndas–16 & 34)

- Upendra Bhanja–Lãvanyabati (Chhãndas–1 & 2).
- (Modern)
- Rãdhãnath Rãy–Chandrabhãgã.
- Mãyãdhar Mänasinha–Jeevan–ChItã.
- Sãtchidananda Routray–Kabitã–1962.
- Ramãkãnta Ratha–Saptama Ritu.

Section B: Drama

- Manoranjan Dãs–Kätha-Ghoda.
- Bijay Mishra—Tata Niranjanä.

Novel:

- Fakir Mohan Senãpati–Chhamãna Ãthaguntha.
- Gopinãth Mohãnty–Dãnãpani.

Short Story:

- Surendra Mohãnty–Marãlara Mrityu.
- Manoj Dãs–Laxmira Abhisãra.

Essay:

- Chittaranjan Dãs–Tranga O Tadit (First Five essays).
- Chandra Sekhar Rath–Mun Satyadharmã Kahuchhi (First five essays).

PUNJABI

Paper-I

Answers must be written in Punjabi in Gurumukhi script

Section A

- Origin of Punjabi Language; different stages of development and recent development in Punjabi Language; characteristics of Punjabi phonology and the study of its tones; classification of vowels and consonants.
- Punjabi morphology; the number-gender system (animate and inanimate), prefixes, affixes and different categories of Post positions; Punjabi word formation; **Tatsam. Tad Bhav.** forms; Sentence structure, the notion of subject and object in Punjabi; Noun and verb phrases.
- **Language and dialect:** the notions of dialect and idiolect: major dialects of Punjabi: Pothohari, Majhi, Doabi, Malwai, Paudhi; the validity of speech variation on the basis of social stratification, the distinctive features of various dialects with special reference to tones Language and script; origin and development of Gurumukhi; Suitability of Gurumukhi for Punjabi.
- **Classical background:** Nath Jogi Sahit.
- **Medieval Literature:** Gurmat, Suti, Kissa and Var: janamsakhis.

Section B

- Modern trends Mystic, romantic, progressive and neomystic (Vir Singh, Puran Singh, Mohan Singh, Amrita Pritam, Bawa Balwant, Pritam Singh Safeer, J. S. Neki).

  Experimentalist (Jasbir Singh Ahluwalia, Ravinder Ravi, Ajaib Kamal).

  Aesthetes (Harbhajan Singh, Tara Singh). Neo-progressive (Pash, Jagtar, Patar).
- Folk Literature Folk songs, Folk tales, Riddles, Proverbs. Epic (Vir Singh, Avtar Singh Azad, Mohan Singh).
- Lyric (Gurus, Sufis and Modern Lyricists-Mohan Singh, Amrita Pritam, Shiv Kumar, Harbhajan Singh).
- Drama (I.C. Nanda, Harcharan Singh, Balwant Gargi, S.S. Sekhon, Charan Das Sidhu).
- Novel (Vir Singh, Nanak Singh, Jaswant Singh Kanwal, K.S. Duggal, Sukhbir, Gurdial Singh, Dalip Kaur Tiwana, Swaran Chandan).

- Short Story (Sujan Singh, K. S. Virk, Prem Parkash, Waryam Sandhu).
- Socio-cultural Sanskrit, Persian and Western. Literary influences;
- Essay (Puran Singh, Teja Singh, Gurbaksh Singh).

Literary Criticism (S.S. Sekhon, Attar Singh, Kishan Singh, Harbhajan Singh, Najam Hussain Sayyad).

Paper-II

Answers must be written in Punjabi in Gurumukhi script

This paper will require first-hand reading of the texts prescribed and will be designed to test the candidate's critical ability.

Section A

- Sheikh Farid The complete Bani as includedin the Adi Granth.
- Guru Nanak Japu Ji. Baramah. Asa di Var.
- Bulleh Shah Kafian
- Waris Shah Heer

Section B

- Shah Mohammad Jangnama (Jang Singhante Firangian)
- Dhani Ram Chatrik Chandan Vari (Poet) Sufi Khana
- Nawan Jahan
- Nanak Singh Chitta Lahu (Novelist) Pavittar Papi
- Ek Mian Do Talwaran
- Gurbaksh Singh Zindagi-di-Ras (Essayist) Nawan Shivala
- Merian Abhul Yadaan. Balraj Sahni Mera Roosi Safarnama
- (Travelogue) Mera Pakistani Safarnama
- Balwant Gargi Loha Kutt (Dramatist) Dhuni-di-Agg
- Sultan Razia Sant Singh Sekhon Sahityarth
- (Critic) Parsidh Punjabi Kavi Punjabi Kav Shiromani.

SANSKRIT

Paper-I

There will be three questions as indicated in the Question Paper which must be answered in Sanskrit. The Remaining questions must be answered either in Sanskrit or in the medium of examination opted by the candidate.

Section–A

- Significant features of the grammar, with particular stress on Sanjna, Sandhi, Karaka, Samasa, Kartari and Karmani vacyas (voice usages) (to be answered in Sanskrit).
- Main characteristics of Vedic Sanskrit language
    - Prominent feature of classical Sanskrit language
    - Contribution of Sanskrit to linguistic studies
- General Knowledge of:—
    - Literary history of Sanskrit
    - Principal trends of literary criticism
    - Ramayana
    - Mahabharata
    - The origin and development of literary geners of: Mahakavya
- Rupaka (drama) Katha
- Akhyayika Campu Khandakavya Muktaka Kavya.

Section–B

- **Essential of Indian Culture with stress on:**
    - Purusãrthas
    - Samskãras
    - Varnãsramavyavasthã
    - Arts and fine arts
    - Technical Sciences.
- **Trends of Indian Philosophy**
    - Mïmansã
    - Vedãnta
    - Nyaya
    - Vaisesika

- Sãnkhya
- Yoga
- Bauddha
- Jaina
- Carvãka

- Short Essay (in Sanskrit)
- Unseen passage with the questions (to be answered in Sanskrit).

Paper-II

Question from Group 4 is to be answered in Sanskrit only. Questions from Groups 1, 2 and 3 are to be answered either in Sanskrit or in the medium opted by the candidate.

Section–A

General study of the following groups: –

Group 1	Raghuvamsam—Kalidasa Kumarasambhavam—Kalidasa Kiratarjuniyam—Bharavi Sisupalavadham—Magha Naisadhiyacaritam—Sriharsa Kadambari—Banabhatta Dasakumaracaritam—Dandin Sivarajyodayam—S.B. Varnekar
Group 2	Isãvãsyopanisad Bhagavadgitã Sundarakanda of Valmiki's Ramayana Arthasastra of Kautilya
Group 3	Svapanavasavadattam—Bhasa Abhijnanasakuntalam—Kalidasa Mricchakatikam—Sudraka Mudraraksasam—Visakhadatta Uttararamacaritam—Bhavbhuti Ratnavali Sriharshavardhana Venisamharam—Bhattanarayana

Contd...

Group 4	❍ Short notes in Sanskrit on the following:— ❍ Meghadutam—Kalidasa ❍ Nitisatakam—Bhartrhari ❍ Pancatantra— ❍ Rajatarangini—Kalhana ❍ Harsacaritam—Banabhatta ❍ Amarukasatakam—Amaruka ❍ Gitagovindam—Jayadeva.

Section-B

This section will require first hand reading of the following selected texts:—(Questions from Groups 1 & 2 are to be answered in Sanskrit only) Questions from Groups 3 and 4 are to be answered either in Sanskrit or in the Medium opted by the candidate.

Group 1	❍ Raghuvamsam—Cantol, Verses 1 to 10 Kumarasambhavam—Canto I, Verses 1 to 10 ❍ Kiratarjuniyaue—Canto I, Verses 1 to 10
Group 2	❍ Isavasyopanisad—Verses—1, 2, 4, 6, 7, 15 and 18 ❍ Bhagavatgita II Chapter Verses13 to 25 ❍ Sundarakandam of Valmiki Canto15, Verses 15 to 30 (Geeta Press Edition)
Group 3	❍ Meghadutam—Verses 1 to 10 ❍ Nitisatakam—Verses 1 to 10 (Edited by D.D. Kosambi Bharatiya Vidya Bhavan Publication) ❍ Kadambari—Sukanasopadesa (only)
Group 4	❍ Svapnavasavadattam Act VI ❍ Abhijnansakuntalam Act IV Verses 15 to 30 (M.R. Kale Edition) ❍ Uttararamacaritam Act I Verses 31 to 47 (M.R. Kale Edition).

SANTHALI

Paper I

Section A

Part I—History of Santhali Language

- Main Austric Language family, population and distribution.
- Grammatical structure of Santhali Language.
- Important character of Santhali Language: Phonology, Morphology, Syntax, Semantics, Translation, Lexicography.
- Impact of other languages of Santhali.
- Standardization of Santhali Language.

Part II—History of Santhali Literature

- Literary trend of the following four periods of history of Santhali Literature.
    - Ancient Literature before 1854.
    - Missionary period Literature between 1855 to 1889 AD.
    - Medieval period: Literature between 1890 to 1946 AD.
    - Modern period: Literature from 1947 AD to till date.
- Writing tradition in History of Santhali literature.

Section-B

Literary forms—Main characteristics, history and development of following literary forms.

Part I

Folk Literature in Santhali folk song, folk tale, phrase, idioms puzzles, and Kudum.

Part II

Modern literature in Santhali

- Development of poetry and prominent poets.
- Development of prose and prominent writers.
    - Novels and prominent Novelists.
    - Stories and prominent story writers.

- Drama and Prominent Dramatist.
- Criticism and prominent critics.
- Essay, sketches, memoirs, travelogues and prominent writers.

Santhali writers

Shyam Sundar Hembram, Pandit Raghunath Murmu, Barha Beshra, Sadhu Ramchand Murmu, Narayan Soren 'Toresutam', Sarda Prasad Kisku, Raghunath Tudu, Kalipada Soren, Sakla Soren, Digamber Hansda, Aditya Mitra 'Santhali', Babulal Murmu 'Adivasi', Jadumani Beshra, Arjun Hembram, Krishna Chandra Tudu, Rupchand Hansda, Kalendra Nath Mandi, Mahadev, Hansda, Gour Chandra Murmu, Thakur Prasad Murmu, Hara Prasad Murmu, Uday Nath Majhi, Parimal Hembram, Dhirendra Nath Baske, Shyam Charan Hembram, Damayanti Beshra, T.K. Rapaj, Boyha Biswanath Tudu.

Part III

Cultural Heritage of Santhali tradition, customs, festival and rituals (birth, marriage and death).

Paper II

Section A

This paper will require in-depth reading of the following texts and the questions will be designed to test the candidates' critical ability.

Ancient Literature:

Prose

- Kherwal Bonso Dhorom Puthi—Majhi Ramdas Tudu "Rasika".
- Mare Hapramko Reyak Katha—L.O. Scrafsrud.
- Jomsim Binti Lita—Mangal Chandra Turkulumang Soren.
- Marang Buru Binti—Kanailal Tudu.

Poetry

- Karam Sereng—Nunku Soren.
- Devi Dasain Sereng—Manindra Hansda.
- Horh Sereng—W.G. Archer.
- Baha Sereng—Balaram Tudu.

- Dong Sereng—Padmashri Bhagwat Murmu 'Thakur'.
- Hor Sereng—Raghunath Murmu.
- Soros Sereng—Babulal Murmu "Adivasi".
- More Sin More Ndia—Rup Chand Hansda.
- Judasi Madwa Latar—Tez Narayan Murmu.

Section-B

Modern Literature

Part I—Poetry

- Onorhen Baha Dhalwak—Paul Jujhar Soren.
- Asar Binti—Narayan Soren "Tore Sutam".
- Chand Mala—Gora Chand Tudu.
- Onto Baha Mala—Aditya Mitra "Santhali".
- Tiryo Tetang—Hari Har Hansda.
- Sisirjon Rar—Thakur Prasad Murmu.

Part II—Novels

- Harmawak Ato—R.Karstiars (Translator—R.K. Kisku Rapaz).
- Manu Mati—Chandra Mohan Hansda.
- Ato Orak—Doman Hansdak.
- Ojoy Gada Dhiph re—Nathenial Murmu.

Part III—Stories

- Jiyon Gada—Rup Chand Hansda and Jadumani Beshra.
- Mayajaal—Doman Sahu 'Samir' and Padmashri Bhagwat Murmu 'Thakur'.

Part IV—Drama

- Kherwar Bir—Pandit Raghunath Murmu.
- Juri Khatir—Dr. K.C. Tudu.
- Birsa Bir—Ravi Lal Tudu.

Part V—Biography

Santal Ko Ren Mayam Gohako—Dr. Biswanath Hansda.

SINDHI

(Can be written in Sindhi, Arabic or Devanagari Script)

Paper I

Section A

- Origin and evolution of Sindhi language—views of different scholars.
- Significant linguistic features of Sindhi language, including those pertaining to its phonology, morphology and syntax.
- Major dialects of the Sindhi language.
- Sindhi vocabulary—stages of its growth, including those in the pre-partition and post-partition periods.
- Historical study of various Writing Systems (Scripts) of Sindhi.
- Changesin the structure of Sindhi language in India, after partition, due to influence of other languages and social conditions.

Section-B

Sindhi literature through the ages in context of socio-cultural conditions in the respective periods:

- Early medieval literature upto 1350 A.D. including folk literature.
- Late medieval period from 1350 A.D. to 1850 A.D.
- Renaissance period from 1850 A.D. to 1947 A.D.
- Modern period from 1947 and onwards.

(Literary genres in Modern Sindhi literature and experiments in poetry, drama, novel, short story, essay, literary criticism, biography, autobiography, memoirs and travelogues.)

Paper II

This paper will require the first-hand reading of the texts prescribed and will be designed to test the candidate's critical ability.

Section-A

References to context and critical appreciation of the texts included in this section.

Poetry

- "Shah Jo Choond Shair": ed. H.I. Sadarangani, Published by Sahitya Akademi (First 100 pages).
- "Sachal Jo Choond Kalam": ed. Kalyan B. Advani Published by Sahitya Akademi (Kafis only).
- "Sami-a-ja Choond Sloka": ed. B.H. Nagrani Published by Sahitya Akademi (First 100 pages).
- "Shair-e-Bewas": by Kishinchand Bewas ("Saamoondi Sipoon" portion only).
- "Roshan Chhanvro": Narayan Shyam.
- "Virhange Khapoi je Sindhi Shair jee Choond": ed. H.I. Sadarangani, published by Sahitya Akademi.

Drama

- "Behtareen Sindhi Natak" (One-act Plays): Edited by M. Kamal Published by Gujarat Sindhi Academy.
- "Kako Kaloomal" (Full-length Play): by Madan Jumani.

Section–B

References to context and critical appreciation of the texts included in this section.

- 'Pakheeara Valar Khan Vichhrya' (Novel): by Gobind Malhi.
- 'Sat Deenhan' (Novel): by Krishin Khatwani.
- 'Choond Sindhi Kahanyoon' (Short Stories) Vol. III.: Edited by Prem Prakash, published by Sahitya Akademi.
- 'Bandhan' (Short Stories): Sundari Uttamchandani.
- 'Behtareen Sindhi Mazmoon' (Essays): Edited by Hiro Thakur, published by Gujarat Sindhi Academi.
- 'Sindhi Tanqeed' (Criticism): Edited by Harish Vaswani: Published by Sahitya Akademi.
- 'Mumhinjee Hayati-a-ja Sona Ropa varqa' (Autobiography): by Popati Hiranandani.
- "Dr. Choithram Gidwani" (Biography): by Vishnu Sharma.

TAMIL

Paper I

Section A

Part 1: History of Tamil Language

- Major Indian Language Families—The place of Tamil among Indian Languages in general and Dravidian in particular—Enumeration and Distribution of Dravidian languages.
- The language of Sangam Literature—The language of medieval Tamil: Pallava Period only—Historical study of Nouns, Verbs, Adjectives, Adverbs—Tense markers and case markers in Tamil.
- Borrowing of words from other languages into Tamil—Regional and social dialects—difference between literary and spoken Tamil.

Part 2: History of Tamil Literature

Tolkappiyam-Sangam Literature—The division of Akam and Puram—The secular characteristics of Sangam Literature—The development of Ethical literature—Silappadikaram and Manimekalai.

Part 3: Devotional Literature (Alwars and Nayanamars)

- The bridal mysticism in Alwar hymns—Minor literary forms (Tutu, Ula, Parani, Kuravanji). Social factors for the development of Modern Tamil Literature; Novel, Short Story and New
- Poetry—The impact of various political ideologies on modern writings.

Section–B

Part 1: Recent trends in Tamil Studies

Approaches to criticism: Social, psychological, historical and moralistic—the use of criticism—the various techniques in literature; Ullurai, Iraicchi, Thonmam (Myth) Otturuvagam (allegory), Angadam (Satire), Meyappadu, Padimam (image), Kuriyeedu (Symbol), Irunmai (Ambiguity)—The concept of comparative literature-the principle of comparative literature.

Part 2: Folk Literature in Tamil

Ballads, Songs, proverbs and riddles—Sociological study of Tamil folklore. Uses of translation—Translation of Tamil works into other languages-Development of journalism in Tamil.

Part 3: Cultural Heritage of the Tamils

Concept of Love and War—Concept of Aram-the ethical codes adopted by the ancient Tamils in their warfare-customs beliefs, rituals, modes of worship in the five Thinais.

The Cultural changes as revealed in post sangam literature—cultural fusion in the medieval period (Janism and Buddhism). The development of arts and architecture through the ages (Pallavas, later Cholas, and Nayaks). The impact of various political, social, religious and cultural movements on Tamil Society. The role of mass media in the cultural change of contemporary Tamil society.

Paper II

The paper will require first-hand reading of the text prescribed and will be designed to test the critical ability of the candidate.

Section–A

Part 1: Ancient Literature

- Kuruntokai (1—25 poems)
- Purananuru (182—200 poems)
- Tirukkural Porutpal: Arasiyalum Amaichiyalum (from Iraimatchi to Avaianjamai).

Part 2: Epic Literature

- Silappadikaram: Madhurai Kandam only.
- Kambaramayanam: Kumbakarunan Vadhai Padalam.

Part 3: Devotional Literature

- Tiruvasagam: Neetthal Vinnappam
- Tiruppavai: (Full Text).

Section–B

Modern Literature

Part 1: Poetry

- Bharathiar: Kannan Pattu

- Bharathidasan: Kudumba Vilakku
- Naa. Kamarasan: Karappu Malarkal

Prose

- Mu. Varadharajanar: Aramum Arasiyalum
- C. N. Annadurai: Ye! Thazhntha Tamilagame.

Part 2: Novel, Short Story and Drama

- Akilon ; Chittairappavai
- Jayakanthan: Gurupeedam
- Cho: Yaurkkum Vetkamillai

Part 3: Folk Literature

- Muthuppattan kathai Edited by Na. Vanamamalai, (Publication: Madurai Kamaraj University).
- Malaiyaruvi, Edited by Ki. Va Jagannathan (Publication: Saraswathi Mahal, Thanjavur).

TELUGU

Paper I

Section A: Language

- Place of Telugu among Dravidian languages and its antiquity—Etymological History of Telugu,Tenugu and Andhra.
- Major linguistic changes in phonological, morphological, grammatical and syntactical levels, from Proto-Dravidian to old Telugu and from old Telugu to Modern Telugu.
- Evolution of spoken Telugu when compared to classical Telugu-Formal and functional view of Telugu language.
- Influence of other languages and its impact on Telugu.
- **Modernization of Telugu language:**
  - Linguistic and literary movements and their role in modernization of Telugu.
  - Role of media in modernization of Telugu (News-papers, Radio, TV etc.)
  - Problems of terminology and mechanisms in coining new terms in Telugu in various discourses including scientific and technical.
- Dialects of Telugu—Regional and social variations and problems of Standardization.
- Syntax—Major divisions of Telugu sentences—simple, complex and compound sentences—Noun and verb predications—Processes of nominalization and relativization—Direct and indirect reporting-conversion processes.
- Translation—Problems of translation, cultural, social and idiomatic—Methods of translation—Approaches to translation—Literary and other kinds of translation—Various uses of translation.

Section B: Literature

- Literature in Pre-Nannaya Period—Marga and Desi poetry.
- Nannaya Period—Historical and literary background of Andhra Mahabharata.
- Saiva poets and their contribution—Dwipada, Sataka, Ragada, Udaharana.
- Tikkana and his place in Telugu literature.
- Errana and his literary works—Nachana Somana and his new approach to poetry.
- Srinatha and Potana—Their works and contribution.
- Bhakti poets in Telugu literature—Tallapaka Annamayya, ramadasu, tyagayya.
- Evolution of prabandhas—Kavya and prabandha.

- Southern school of Telugu literature-raghunatha Nayaka, chemakura vankatakavi and women poets-Literary forms like yakshagana, prose and padakavita.
- Modern Telugu Literature and literary forms—Novel, Short Story, Drama, Playlet and poetic forms.
- Literary Movements : Reformation, Nationalism, Neo-classisicism, Romanticism and Progressive, Revolutionary movements.
- Digambarakavulu, feminist and dalit Literature.
- Main divisions of folk literature—Performing folk arts.

Paper II

This paper will require first hand reading of the prescribed texts and will be designed to test the candidate's critical ability, which will be in relation to the following approaches:—

- Aesthetic approach—Rassa, Dhawani, Vakroti and Auchitya—Formal and Structural-Imagery and Symbolism.
- Sociological, Historical, Ideological, Psychological approaches.

Section-A

- Nannaya-Dushyanta Chritra (Adiparva 4th Canto verses 5—109).
- Tikkana-Sri Krishna Rayabaramu (Udyoga parva-3rd Canto verses 1—144).
- Srinath-Guna Nidhi Katha (Kasikhandam, 4th Canto, verses 76—133).
- Pingali Surana-sugatri Salinulakatha (Kalapurno-dayamu 4 Canto verses, 60—142).
- Molla-Ramayanamu (Balakanda including avatarika).
- Kasula Purushothama Kavi—Andhra Nayaka Satakamu.

Section-B

- Gurajada Appa Rao—Animutyalu (Short stories).
- Viswanatha Satyanarayana—Andhra prasasti.
- Devulapalli Krishna Sastry—Krishnapaksham (excluding Uravsi and Pravasam).
- Sri Sri-Maha prastanam.
- Jashuva-Gabbilam (Part I).
- C. Narayana Reddy—Karpuravasanta rayalu.
- Kanuparti Varalakshmamma—Sarada lekhalu (Part I).
- Atreya—N.G.O.
- Racha Konda Viswanatha Sastry—Alpajaeevi.

URDU

Paper I

Section A

Development of Urdu Language

- Development of Indo-Aryan
  - Old Indo-Aryan
  - Middle Indo-Aryan
  - New Indo-Aryan.
- Western Hindi and its dialects Brij Bhasha Khadi Boli, Haryanavi, Kannauji, Bundeli—Theories about the origin of Urdu language.
- Dakhani Urdu—origin and development, its significant linguistic features.
- Social and Cultural roots of Urdu language— and its distinctive features. Script, Phonology, Morphology, Vocabulary.

Section–B

- **Genres and their development:**
  - **Poetry:** Ghazal, Masnavi, Qasida, Marsia, Rubai Jadid Nazm.
  - **Prose:** Novel, Short Story, Dastan, Drama, Inshaiya, Khutoot, Biography.
- Significant feaures of: (i) Deccani, Delhi and Lucknow schools, (ii) Sir Syed movement, Romantic movement, Progressive movement, Modernism.
- Literary Criticism and its development with reference to Hali, Shibli, Kaleemuddin Ahmad, Ehtisham Hussain, Ale-Ahmad Suroor.
- Essay writing (covering literary and imaginativetopics).

Paper II

Answer must be written in Urdu

This paper will require first hand reading of the texts prescribed and will be designed to test the candidate's critical ability.

Section–A		
1.	Mir Amman	Bagho-Babar
2.	Ghalib	Intikhab-e-Khutoot-e Ghalib
3.	Mohd. Husain Azad	Nairang-e-Khayal
4.	Prem Chand	Godan
5.	Rajendra Singh Bedi	Apne Dukh Mujhe Dedo
6.	Abul Kalam Azad	Ghubar-e-Khatir
Section–B		
1.	Mir	Intikhab-e-Kalam-e-Mir (Ed. Abdul Haq.)
2.	Mir Hasan	Sahrul Bayan
3.	Ghalib	Diwan-e-Ghalib
4.	Iqbal	Bal-e-Jibrail
5.	Firaq	Gul-e-Naghma
6.	Faiz	Dast-e-Saba
7.	Akhtruliman	Bint-e-Lamhat

MANAGEMENT

The candidate should make a study of the concept of development of Management as science and art drawing upon the contributions of leading thinkers of management and apply the concepts to the real life of government and business decision-making keeping in view the changes in the strategic and operative environment.

Paper I

Managerial Function and Process

Concept and foundations of management, Evolution of Management Thoughts; Managerial Functions—Planning, Organizing, Controlling; Decision-making; Role of Manager, Managerial skills; Entrepreneurship; Management of innovation; Managing in a global environment, Flexible Systems Management; Social responsibility and managerial ethics; Process and customer orientation; Managerial processes on direct and indirect value chain.

Organisational Behaviour and Design

Conceptual model of organization behaviour; The individual processes—personality, values and attitude, perception, motivation, learning and reinforcement, work stress and stress management; The dynamics of Organization behaviour—power and politics, conflict and negotiation, leadership process and styles, communication; The Organizational Processes—decision-making, job design; Classical, Neoclassical and Contingency approaches to organizational design; Organizational theory and design—Organizational culture, managing cultural diversity, learning Organization; Organizational change and development; Knowledge Based Enterprise—systems and processes; Networked and virtual organizations.

Human Resource Management

HR challenges; HRM functions; The future challenges of HRM; Strategic Management of human resources; Human resource planning; Job analysis; Job evaluation, Recruitment and selection; Training and development; Promotion and transfer; Performance management; Compensation management and bnenefits; Employee morale and productivity; Management of Organizational climate and Industrial relations; Human resources accounting and audit; Human resource information system; International human resource management.

Accounting for Managers

Financial accounting—concept, importance and scope, generally accepted accounting principles, preparation of financial statements with special reference to analysis of a balance sheet and measurment of business income, inventory valuation and depreciation, financial statement analysis, fund flow analysis, the statement of cash flows; Management accounting concept, need, imporance and scope; Cost accounting—records and processes, cost ledger and control accounts, reconciliation and integration bwtween financial and cost accounts; Overhead cost and control, Job and process costing, Budget and budgetary control, Performance budgeting, Zero-base budgeting, relevant costing and costing for decision-making, standard costing and variance analysis, marginal costing and absorption costing.

Financial Management

Goal of Finance Function. Concepts of value and return. Valuation of bonds and Shares; Management of working capital: Estimation and Financing; Management of cash, receivables, inventory and current liabilities; Cost of capital ; Capital budgeting; Financial and operating leverage; Design of capital structure: theories and practices; Shareholder value creation: dividend policy, corporate financial policy and strategy, management of corporate distress and restructuring strategy; Capital and money markets: institutions and instruments; Leasing hire purchase and venture capital; Regulation of capital market; Risk and return: portfolio theory; CAPM; APT; Financial derivatives: option, futures, swap; Recent reforms in financial sector.

Marketing Management

Concept, evolution and scope; Marketing strategy formulation and components of marketing plan; Segmenting and targeting the market; Positioning and differentiating the market offering; Analyzing competition; Analyzing consumer markets; Industrial buyer behaviour; Market research; Product strategy; Pricing strategies; Designing and managing Marketing channels; Integrated marketing communications; Building customer staisfaction, Value and retention; Services and non-profit marketing; Ethics in marketing; Consumer protection; Internet marketing; Retail management; Customer relationship management; Concept of holistic marketing.

Paper-II

Quantitative Techniques in Decision-making

Descriptive statistics—tabular, graphical and numerical methods, introduction to probability, discrete and continuous probability distributions, inferential statistics-sampling distributions, central limit theorem, hypothesis testing for differences between means and proportions, inference about population variances, Chisquare and ANOVA, simple correlation and regression, time series and forecasting, decision theory, index numbers; Linear programming—problem formulation, simplex method and graphical solution, sensitivity analysis.

Production and Operations Management

Fundamentals of operations management; Organizing for production; Aggregate production planning, capacity planning, plant design: process planning, plant size and scale of operations, Management of facilities; Line balancing; Equipment replacement and maintenance; Production control; Supply, chain management—vendor evaluation and audit; Quality management; Statistical process control, Six Sigma; Flexibility and agility in manufacturing systems; World class manufaturing; Project management concepts, R&D management, Management of service operations; Role and importance of materials management, value analysis, make or buy decision; Inventory control, MRP; Waste management.

Management Information System

Conceptual foundations of information systems; Information theory; Information resource management; Types of information Systems; Systems Development—Overview of Systems and Design; System Development management life-cycle, Designing online and distributed environments; Implementation and control of project; Trends in information technology; Managing data resources—Organising data. DSS and RDBMS; Enterprise Resource Planning (ERP), Expert systems, e-Business architecture, e-Governance; Information systems planning, Flexibility in information systems; User involvement; Evaluation of information systems.

Government Business Interface

State participation in business, Interaction between Government, Business and different Chambers of Commerce and Industry in India; Government's ploicy with regard to Small Scale Industries; Government clearances for establishing a new enterprise; Public Distribution System; Government control over price and distribution; Consumer Protection Act (CPA) and The Role of Voluntary Organizations in protecting consumers' rights; New Industrial Policy of the Government: liberalization, deregulation and privatisation; Indian planning system; Government policy concerning development of Backward areas/regions; The Responsibilities of the business as well as the Government to protect the environment; Corporate Governance; Cyber Laws.

Strategic Cost Management

Business policy as a field of study; Nature and scope of strategic management, Strategic intent, vision, objectives and policies; Process of strategic planning and implementa-tion; Environmental analysis and internal analysis; SWOT analysis; Tools and techniques for strategic analysis—Impact matrix: The experience curve, BCG matrix, GEC mode, Industry analysis, Concept of value chain; Strategic profile of a firm; Framework for analysing competition; Competitive advantage of a firm; Generic competitive strategies; Growth strategies—expansion, integration and diversification; Concept of core competence, Strategic flexibility; Reinventing strategy; Strategy and structure; chief Executive and Board; turnaround management; Management of strategic change; Strategic alliances, Mergers and Acquisitions; Strategy and corporate evolution in the Indian context.

International Business

International Business Environment: Changing composition of trade in goods and services; India's Foreign Trade: Policy and trends; Financing of International trade; Regional Economic Cooperation; FTAs; Internationalisation of service firms; International production; Operation Management in International companies; International Taxation; Global competitiveness and technological developments; Global E-Business; Designing global organisational structure and control; Multicultural management; Global business strategy; Global marketing strategies; Export Management; Export-Import procedures; Joint Ventures; Foreign Investment: Foreign direct investment and foreign portfolio investment; Cross-border Mergers and Acquisitions; Foreign Exchange Risk Exposure Management; World Financial Markets and International Banking; External Debt Management; Country Risk Analysis.

MATHEMATICS

Paper–I

Linear Algebra

- Vector spaces over R and C, linear dependence and independence, subspaces, bases, dimensions, Linear transformations, rank and nullity, matrix of a linear transformation.
- Algebra of Matrices; Row and column reduction, Echelon form, congruence's and similarity; Rankof a matrix; Inverse of a matrix; Solution of system of linear equations; Eigenvalues and eigenvectors, characteristic polynomial, Cayley-Hamilton theorem, Symmetric, skew-symmetric, Hermitian, skew-Hermitian, orthogonal and unitary matrices and their eigenvalues.

Calculus

- Real numbers, functions of a real variable, limits, continuity, differentiability, mean-value theorem, Taylor's theorem with remainders, indeterminate forms, maxima and minima, asymptotes; Curve tracing; Functions of two or three variables; Limits, continuity, partial derivatives, maxima and minima, Lagrange's method of multipliers, Jacobian.
- Riemann's definition of definite integrals; Indefinite integrals; Infinite and improper integral; Double and triple integrals (evaluation techniques only); Areas, surface and volumes.

Analytic Geometry

Cartesian and polar coordinates in three dimensions, second degree equations in three variables, reduction to Canonical forms, straight lines, shortest distance between two skew lines, Plane, sphere, cone, cylinder, paraboloid, ellipsoid, hyperboloid of one and two sheets and their properties.

Ordinary Differential Equations

- Formulation of differential equations; Equations of first order and first degree, integrating factor; Orthogonal trajectory, Equations of first order but not of first degree, Clairaut's equation, singular solution.
- Second and higher order liner equations with constant coefficients, complementary function, particular integral and general solution.

- Section order linear equations with variable coefficients, Euler-Cauchy equation; Determination of complete solution when one solution is known using method of variation of parameters.
- Laplace and Inverse Laplace transforms and their properties, Laplace transforms of elementary functions. Application to initial value problems for 2nd order linear equations with constant coefficients.

Dynamics and Statics

- Rectilinear motion, simple harmonic motion, motion in a plane, projectiles; Constrained motion; Work and energy, conservation of energy; Kepler's laws, orbits under central forces.
- Equilibrium of a system of particles; Work and potential energy, friction, Common catenary; Principle of virtual work; Stability of equilibrium, equilibrium of forces in three dimensions.

Vector Analysis

- Scalar and vector fields, differentiation of vector field of a scalar variable; Gradient, divergence and curl in cartesian and cylindrical coordinates; Higher order derivatives; Vector identities and vector equation.
- Application to geometry: Curves in space, curvature and torsion; Serret-Furenet's formulae. Gauss and Stokes' theorems, Green's indentities.

Paper–II

Algebra

- Groups, subgroups, cyclic groups, cosets, Lagrange's Theorem, normal subgroups, quotient groups, homomorphism of groups, basic isomorphism theorems, permutation groups, Cayley's theorem.
- Rings, subrings and ideals, homomorphisms of rings; Integral domains, principal ideal domains, Euclidean domains and unique factorization domains; Fields, quotient fields.

Real Analysis

- Real number system as an ordered field with least upper bound property; Sequences, limit of a sequence, Cauchy sequence, completeness of real line; Series and its convergence, absolute and conditional convergence of series of real and complex terms, rearrangement of series. Continuity and uniform continuity of functions, properties of continuous functions on compact sets.

- Riemann integral, improper integrals; Fundamental theorems of integral calculus.
- Uniform convergence, continuity, differentiability and integrability for sequences and series of functions; Partial derivatives of functions of several (two or three) variables, maxima and minima.

Complex Analysis

Analytic function, Cauchy-Riemann equations, Cauchy's theorem, Cauchy's integral formula, power series, representation of an analytic function, Taylor's series; Singularities; Laurent's series; Cauchy's residue theorem; Contour integration.

Linear Programming

Linear programming problems, basic solution, basic feasible solution and optimal solution; Graphical method and simplex method of solutions; Duality.

Transportation and assignment problems.

Partial Differential Equations

Family of surfaces in three dimensions and formulation of partial differential equations; Solution of quasilinear partial differential equations of the first order, Cauchy's method of characteristics; Linear partial differential equations of the second order with constant coefficients, canonical form; Equation of a vibrating string, heat equation, Laplace equation and their solutions.

Numerical Analysis and Computer Programming

- Numerical methods: Solution of algebraic and transcendental equations of one variable by bisection, Regula-Falsi and Newton-Raphson methods, solution of system of linear equations by Gaussian Elimination and Gauss-Jorden (direct), Gauss-Seidel (iterative) methods. Newton's (forward and backward) and interpolation, Lagrange's interpolation.
- Numerical integration: Trapezoidal rule, Simpson's rule, Gaussian quadrature formula. Numerical solution of ordinary differential equations: Eular and Runga Kutta methods.
- Computer Programming: Binary system; Arithmetic and logical operations on numbers; Octal and Hexadecimal Systems; Conversion to and from decimal Systems; Algebra of binary numbers.

- Elements of computer systems and concept of memory; Basic logic gates and truth tables, Boolean algebra, normal forms.
- Representation of unsigned integers, signed integers and reals, double precision reals and long integers.
- Algorithms and flow charts for solving numerical analysis problems.

Mechanics and Fluid Dynamics

- Generalised coordinates; D'Alembert's principle and Lagrange's equations; Hamilton equations; Moment of inertia; Motion of rigid bodies in two dimensions.
- Equation of continuity; Euler's equation of motion for inviscid flow; Stream-lines, path of a particle; Potential flow; Two-dimensional and axisymmetric motion; Sources and sinks, vortex motion; Navier-Stokes equation for a viscous fluid.

MECHANICAL ENGINEERING

Paper–I

Mechanics of Rigid Bodies

Equations of equilibrium in space and its application; first and second moments of area; simple problems on friction; kinematics of particles for plane motion; elementary particle dynamics.

Mechanics of Deformable Bodies

Generalized Hooke's law and its application; design problems on axial stress, shear stress and bearing stress; material properties for dynamic loading; bending shear and stresses in beams; determination of principle stresses and strains-analytical and graphical; compound and combined stresses; bi-axial stresses-thin walled pressure vessel; material behaviour and design factors for dynamic load; design of circular shafts for bending and torsional load only; deflection of beam for statically determinate problems; theories of failure.

Engineering Materials

Basic concepts on structure of solids, common ferrous and non-ferrous materials and their applications; heat-treatment of steels; non-metalsplastics, cermics, composite materials and nano-materials.

Theory of Machines

Kinematic and dynamic analysis of plane mechanisms. Cams, Gears and empicyclie gear trains, flywheels, governors, balancing of rigid rotors, balancing of single and multicy- linder engines, linear vibration analysis of mechanical systems (single degree of freedom), Critical speeds and whirling of shafts.

Manufacturing Science

Manufacturing Process:

- Machine tool engineering - Merhant's force analysis: Taylor's tool life equation; conventional machining; NC and CNC machining process; jigs and fixtures.
- Non-conventional machining-EDM, ECM, ultrasonic, water jet machining etc.; application of lasers and plasmas; energy rate calculations.
- Forming and welding processes-standard processes.
- Metrology-concept of fits and tolerances; tools and guages; comparators; inspection of length; position; profile and surface finish.

Manufacturing Management

- System design: factory location—simple OR models; plant layout-methods based; applications of engineering economic analysis and break-even analysis for product selection, process selection and capacity planning; predetermined time standards.
- System planning; forecasting methods based on regression and decomposition, design and blancing of multi model and stochastic assembly lines; inventory management-probablistic inventory models for order time and order quanitity determination; JIT systems; strategic sourcing; managing inter plant logistics.
- System operations and control: Scheduling algorithms for job shops; applications of statistical methods for product and process quality control applications of control charts for mean, range, percent defective, number of defectives and defects per unit; quality cost systems; management of resources, organizations and risks in projects.
- System improvement: Implementation of systems, such as total quality management, developing and managing flexible, lean and agile Organizations.

Paper–II

Thermodynamics, Gas Dynamics Turbine

- Basic concept of First-law and Second law of Thermodynamics; concept of entropy and reversibility; availability and unavailability and irreversibility.
- Classification and properties of fluids; incompressible and compressible fluids flows; effect of Mach number and compressibility; continuity momentum and energy equations; normal and oblique shocks; one dimensional isentropic flow; flow or fluids in duct with frictions that transfer.
- Flow through fans, blowers and compressors; axial and centrifugal flow configuration; design of fans and compressors; single problems compresses and turbine cascade; open and closed cycle gas turbines; work done in the gas turbine; reheat and regenerators.

Heat Transfer

- Conduction heat transfer—general conduction equation-Laplace, Poisson and Fourier equations; Fourier law of conduction; one dimensional steady state heat conduction applied to simple wall, solid and hollow cylinder and spheres.
- Convection heat transfer—Newton's law of convection; free and forces convection; heat transfer during laminar and turbulent flow of an incompressible fluid over a flat plate; concepts of Nusselt number, hydrodynamic and thermal boundary layer their thickness; Prandtl number; analogy between heat and momentum transfer—Reynolds, Colbum, Prandtl analogies; heat transfer during

laminar and turbulent flow through horizontal tubes; free convection from horizontal and vertical plates.

- Black body radiation—basic radiation laws such as Stefan-boltzman, Planck distribution, Wein's displacement etc.
- Basic heat exchanger analysis; classification of heat exchangers.

Engines

- Classification, themodynamic cycles of operation; determination of break power, indicated power, mechanical efficiency, heat balance sheet, interpretation of performance characteristics, petrol, gas and diesel engines.
- Combustion in SI and CI engines, normal and abnormal combustion; effect of working parameters on knocking, reduction of knocking; Forms of combustion chamber for SI and CI engines; rating of fuels; additives; emission.
- Different systems of IC engines-fuels; lubricating; cooling and transmission systems. Alternate fuels in IC engines.

Steam Engineering:

- Steam generation—modified Ranking cycle analysis; Modern steam boilers; steam at critical and supercritical pressures; draught equipment; natural and artificial draught; boiler fuels solid, liquid and gaseous fuels. Steam turbines—Principle; types; compounding; impulse and reaction turbines; axial thrust.
- Steam nozzles—flow of steam in convergent and divergent nozzle pressure at throat for maximum discharge with different initial steam conditions such as wet, saturated and superheated, effect of variation of back pressure; supersaturated flow of steam in nozzles, Wilson line.
- Rankine cycle with internal and external irreversibility; reheat factor; reheating and regeneration, methods of governing; back pressure and pass out turbines.
- Steam power plants—combined cycle power generation; heat recovery steam generators (HRSG) fired and unfired, co-generation plants.

Refrigeration and Air-conditioning

- Vapour compression refrigeration cycle—cycle on p-H & T-s diagrams; ecofriendly refrigerants—R 134a. 123; Systems like evaporators, condensers, compressor, expansion devices. Simple vapour absorption systems.
- Psychrometry properties; processes; charts; sensible heating and cooling; humidification and dehumidification effective temperature; air-conditioning load calculation; simple duct design.

MEDICAL SCIENCE

Paper–I

Human Anatomy

- Applied anatomy including blood and nerve supply of upper and lower limbs and joints of shoulder, hip and knee.
- Gross anatomy, blood supply and lymphatic drainage of tongue, thyroid, mammary gland, stomach, liver, prostate, gonads and uterus.
- Applied anatomy of diaphragm, perineum and inguinal region.
- Clinical anatomy of kidney, urinary bladder, uterine tubes, vas deferens.
- **Embryology:** Placenta and placental barrier. Development of heart, gut, kidney. uterus, ovary, testis and their common congenital abnormalities.
- **Central and Peripheral Autonomic Nervous System:** Gross and clinical anatomy of ventricles of brain, circulation of cerebrospinal fluid; Neural pathways and lesions of cutaneous sensations, hearing and vision; Cranial nerves distribution and clinical significance; Components of autonomic nervous system.

Human Physiology

- Conduction and transmission of impulse, mechanism of contraction, neuromuscular transmission, reflexes, control of equilibrium, posture and muscle tone, descending pathways, functions of cerebellum, basal ganglia, Physiology of sleep and consciousness.
- **Endocrine System:** Mechanism of action of hormones; formation, secretion, transport, metabolism, function and regulation of secretion of pancreas and pituitary gland.
- **Physiology of Reproductive System:** Pregnancy menstrual cycle, lactation, pregnancy.
- **Blood:** Development, regulation and fate of blood cells.
- Cardio-vascular,cardiac output, blood pressure, regulation of cardiovascular functions.

Biochemistry

- Organ function tests—liver, kidney, thyroid Protein synthesis. Vitamins and minerals.
- Restriction fragment length. polymorphism (RFLP).
- Polymerase chain reaction (PCR). Radio-immunoassays (RIA).

Pathology

Inflammation and repair, disturbances of growth and cancer, Pathogenesis and histopathology of rheumatic and ischaemic heart disease and diabetes mellitus. Differentiation between benign, malignant, primary and metastatic malignancies, Pathogenesis and histopathology of bronchogenic carcinoma, carcinoma breast, oral cancer, cancer cervix, leukemia, Etiology, pathogenesis and histopathology of—cirrhosis liver, glomerulonephritis, tuberculosis, acute osteomyelitis.

Microbiology

- Humoral and cell mediated immunity.
- Diseases caused by and laboratory diagnosis of —
  - Meningococcus, Saimonella
  - Shigella, Herpes, Dengue, Polio
  - HIV/AIDS, Malaria, E. Histolytica, Giardia
  - Candida, Cryptococcus, Aspergillus.

Pharmacology

Mechanism of action and side effects of the following drugs:

- Antipyretics and analgesics, Antibiotics,
- Antimalaria, Antikala-azar, Antidiabetics,
- Antihypertensive, Antidiuretics, General and cardiac vasodilators, Antiviral, Antiparasitic, Antifungal, Immunosuppressants,
- Anticancer.

Forensic Medicine and Toxicology

Forensic examination of injuries and wounds; Examination of blood and seminal stains; Poisoning, sedative overdose, hanging, drowning, burns, DNA and finger print study.

Paper-II

General Medicine

Etiology, clinical features, diagnosis and principles of management (including prevention) of—Typhoid, Rabies, AIDS, Dengue, Kala-azar, Japanese Encephalitis.

- Etiology, clinical features, diagnosis and principles of management of: Ischaemic heart disease, pulmonary embolism.

- Bronchial asthma.
- Pleural effusion, tuberculosis, Malabsorption syndromes; acid peptic diseases, Viral hepatitis and cirrhosis of liver.

Glomerulonephritis and pyelonephritis, renal failure, nephrotic syndrome, renovascular hypertension, complications of diabetes mellitus, coagulation disorders, leukaemia, Hypo and hyper thyrodism, meningitis and encephalitis.

Imaging in medical problems, ultrasound, echo- cardiogram, CT scan, MRI. Anxiety and Depressive Psychosis and schizophrenia and ECT.

Paediatrics

Immunization, Baby friendly hospital, congenital cyanotic heart disease, respiratory distress syndrome, broncho— pneumonias, kernicterus. IMNCI classification and management, PEM grading and management. ARI and Diarrhea of under five and their management.

Dermatology

Psoriasis, Allergic dermatitis, scabies, eczema, vitiligo, Stevan Johnson's syndrome, Lichen Planus.

General Surgery

- Clinical features, causes, diagnosis and principles of management of cleft palate, harelip. Laryngeal tumour, oral and esophageal tumours.
- Peripheral arterial diseases, varicose veins, coarctation of aorta. Tumours of Thyroid, Adrenal, Glands.
- Abscess cancer, fibroadenoma and adenosis of breast.
- Bleeding peptic ulcer, tuberculosis of bowel, ulcerative colitis, cancer stomach. Renal mass, cancer prostatie.
- Haemothorax, stones of Gall bladder, Kidney, Ureter and Urinary Bladder.
- Management of surgical conditions of Rectum, Anus and Anal canal, Gall bladder and Bile ducts.
- Splenomegaly, cholecystitis, portal hypertension, liver abscess, peritonitis, carcinoma head of pancreas.
- Fractures of spine, Colles' fracture and bone tumors. Endoscopy.
- Laprascopic Surgery.

Obstetrics and Gynaecology including Family Planning

- Diagnosis of pregnancy.
- Labour management, complications of 3rd stage, Antepartum and postpartum hemorrhage, resuscitation of the newborn, Management of abnormal life and difficult labour. Management of small for date or premature newborn.
- Diagnosis and management of anemia. Preeclampsia and Toxaemias of pregnancy, Management of Post- menopausal Syndrome.
- Intra-uterine devices, pills, tubectomy and vasectomy. Medical termination of pregnancy including legal aspects.
- Cancer cervix.
- Leucorrhoea, pelvic pain; infertility, dysfunctional uterine bleeding (DUB), amenorrhoea, Fibroid and prolapse of uterus.

Community Medicine (Preventive and Social Medicine)

- Principles, methods approach and measurements of Epidemiology.
- Nutrition, nutritional diseases/diorders and Nutrition Programmes. Health information Collection, Analysis and Presentation.
- Objectives, components and critical analysis of National programmes for control/ eradication of:
- Malaria, Kala-azar, Filaria and Tuberculosis, HIV/AIDS, STDs and Dengue.
- Critical appraisal of Health care delivery system.
- Health management and administration; Techniques, Tools, Programme Implementation and Evaluation.
- Objectives, Components, Goals and Status of Reproductive and Child Health, National Rural Health Mission and Millennium Development Goals. Management of hospital and industrial waste.

PHILOSOPHY

Paper-I

History and Problems of Philosophy

- Plato and Aristotle: Ideas; Substance; Form and Matter; Causation; Actuality and Potentiality.
- Rationalism (Descartes, Spinoza, Leibniz); Cartesian Method and Certain Knowledge; Substance; God; Mind-Body Dualism; Determinism and Freedom.
- Empiricism (Locke, Berkeley, Hume): Theory of Knowledge; Substance and Qualities; Self and God; Scepticism.
- Kant: Possibility of Synthetic a priori Judgments; Space and Time; Categories; Ideas of Reason; Antinomies; Critique of Proofs for the Existence of God.
- Hegel: Dialectical Method; Absolute Idealism.
- Moore, Russell and Early Wittgenstein: Defence of Commonsense; Refutation of Idealism; Logical Atomism; Logical Constructions; Incomplete Symbols; Picture Theory of Meaning; Sying and Showing.
- Logical Positivism: Verification Theory of Meaning; Rejection of Metaphysics; Linguistic Theory of Necessary Propositions.
- Later Wittgenstein: Meaning and Use; Language-games; Critique of Private Language.
- Phenomenology (Husserl): Method; Theory of Essences; Avoidance of Psychologism.
- Existentialism (Kierkegaard, Sarte, Heidegger): Existence and Essence; Choice, Responsibility and Authentic Existence; Being-in-the-world and Temporality.
- Quine and Strawson: Critique of Empiricism; Theory of Basic Particulars and Persons.
- Carvaka: Theory of Knowlegde; Rejection of Transcendent Entities.
- Jainism: Theory of Reality; Saptabhanginaya; Bondage and Liberation.
- Schools of Buddhism: Prat Ityasamutpada; Ksanikavada, Nairatmyavada.
- Nyaya—Vaiesesika: Theory of Categories; Theory of Appearance; Theory of Pramana; Self, Liberation; God; Proofs for the Existence of God; Theory of Causation; Atomistic Theory of Creation.
- Samkhya; Prakrit; Purusa; Causation; Liberation.
- Yoga; Citta; Cittavrtti; Klesas; Samadhi; Kaivalya.
- Mimamsa: Theory of Knowlegde.

- Schools of Vedanta: Brahman; Isvara; Atman; Jiva; Jagat; Maya; Avida; Adhyasa; Moksa; Aprthaksiddhi; Pancavidhabheda.
- Aurobindo: Evolution, Involution; Integral Yoga.

Paper-II

Socio-Political Philosophy

- Social and Political Ideals: Equality, Justice, Liberty.
- Sovereignty: Austin, Bodin, Laski, Kautilya.
- Individual and State: Rights; Duties and Accountability.
- Forms of Government: Monarchy; Theocracy and Democracy.
- Political Ideologies: Anarchism; Marxism and Socialism.
- Humanism; Secularism; Multi-culturalism.
- Crime and Punishment: Corruption, Mass Violence, Genocide, Capital Punishment.
- Development and Social Progress.
- Gender Discrimination: Female Foeticide, Land and Property Rights; Empowerment.
- Caste Discrimination: Gandhi and Ambedkar.

Philosophy of Religion

- Notions of God: Attributes; Relation to Man and the World. (Indian and Western).
- Proofs for the Existence of God and their Critique (Indian and Western).
- Problem of Evil.
- Soul: Immortality; Rebirth and Liberation.
- Reason, Revelation and Faith.
- Religious Experience: Nature and Object (Indian and Western).
- Religion without God.
- Religion and Morality.
- Religious Pluralism and the Problem of Absolute Truth.
- Nature of Religious Language: Analogical and Symbolic; Cognitivist and Non-cognitive.
  - Mechanics of Particles:

PHYSICS

Paper-I

Mechanics of Particles

Laws of motion; conservation of energy and momentum, applications to rotating frames, centripetal and Coriolis accelerations; Motion under a central force; Conservation of angular momentum, Kepler's laws; Fields and potentials; Gravitational field and potential due to spherical bodies, Gauss and Poisson equations, gravitational self-energy; Two-body problem; Reduced mass; Rutherford scattering; Centre of mass and laboratory reference frames.

Mechanics of Rigid Bodies

System of particles; Centre of mass, angular momentum, equations of motion; Conservation theorems for energy, momentum and angular momentum; Elastic and inelastic collisions; Rigid Body; Degrees of freedom, Euler's theorem, angular velocity, angular momentum, moments of inertia, theorems of parallel and perpendicular axes, equation of motion for rotation; Molecular rotations (as rigid bodies); Di and tri-atomic molecules; Precessional motion; top, gyroscope.

Mechanics of Continuous Media

Elasticity, Hooke's law and elastic constants of isotropic solids and their inter-relation; Streamline (Laminar) flow, viscosity, Poiseuille's equation, Bernoulli's equation, Stokes' law and applications.

Special Relativity

Michelson-Morely experiment and its implications; Lorentz transformations length contraction, time dilation, addition of relativistic velocities, aberration and Doppler effect, mass-energy relation, simple applications to a decay process. Four dimensional momentum vector; Covariance of equations of physics.

Waves and Optics

Waves

Simple harmonic motion, damped oscillation, forced oscillation and resonance; Beats; Stationary waves in a string; Pulses and wave packets; Phase and group velocities; Reflection and refraction from Huygens' principle.

Geometrial Optics

Laws of reflection and refraction from Fermat's principle; Matrix method in paraxial optic-thin lens formula, nodal planes, system of two thin lenses, chromatic and spherical aberrations.

Interference

Interference of light -Young's experiment, Newton's rings, interference by thin films, Michelson interferometer; Multiple beam interference and Fabry Perot interferometer.

Diffraction

Fraunhofer diffraction - single slit, double slit, diffraction grating, resolving power; Diffraction by a circular aperture and the Airy pattern; Fresnel diffraction: half-period zones and zone plates, circular aperture.

Polarisation and Modern Optics

Production and detection of linearly and circularly polarized light; Double refraction, quarter wave plate; Optical activity; Principles of fibre optics, attenuation; Pulse dispersion in step index and parabolic index fibres; Material dispersion, single mode fibers; Lasers-Einstein A and B coefficients. Ruby and He-Ne lasers. Characteristics of laser light-spatial and temporal coherence; Focusing of laser beams. Three-level scheme for laser operation; Holography and simple applications.

Electricity and Magnetism

Electrostatics and Magnetostatics:

Laplace and Poisson equations in electrostatics and their applications; Energy of a system of charges, multipole expansion of scalar potential; Method of images and its applications. Potential and field due to a dipole, force and torque on a dipole in an external field; Dielectrics, polarisation. Solutions to boundary-value problems-conducting and dielectric spheres in a uniform electric field; Magnetic shell, uniformly magnetised sphere; Ferromagnetic materials, hysteresis, energy loss.

Current Electricity

Kirchhoff's laws and their applications. Biot-Savart law, Ampere's law, Faraday's law, Lenz' law. Self-and mutual- inductances; Mean and rms values in AC circuits, DC and AC circuits with R, L and C components; Series and parallel resonance; Quality factor; Principle of transformer.

Electromagnetic Waves and Blackbody Radiation

Displacement current and Maxwell's equations; Wave equations in vacuum, Poynting theorem; Vector and scalar potentials; Electromagnetic field tensor, covariance of Maxwell's equations; Wave equations in isotropic dielectrics, reflection and refraction at the boundary of two dielectrics; Fresnel's relations; Total internal reflection; Normal and anomalous dispersion; Rayleigh scattering; Blackbody radiation and Planck 's radiation law- Stefan-Boltzmann law, Wien's displacement law and Rayleigh-Jeans law.

Thermal and Statistical Physics

- **Thermodynamics:**
  - Laws of thermodynamics, reversible and irreversible processes, entropy; Isothermal, adiabatic, isobaric, isochoric processes and entropy changes; Otto and Diesel engines, Gibbs' phase rule and chemical potential; Van der Waals equation of state of a real gas, critical constants; Maxwell-Boltzmann distribution of molecular velocities, transport phenomena, equipartition and virial theorems; Dulong-Petit, Einstein, and Debye's theories of specific heat of solids; Maxwell relations and application; Clausius-Clapeyron equation. Adiabatic demagnetisation, Joule-Kelvin effect and liquefaction of gases.
- **Statistical Physics:**
  - Macro and micro states, statistical distributions, Maxwell-Boltzmann, Bose-Einstein and Fermi-Dirac Distributions, applications to specific heat of gases and blackbody radiation; Concept of negative temperatures.

Paper-II

Quantum Mechanics

Wave-particle duality; Schroedinger equation and expectation values; Uncertainty principle; Solutions of the one-dimensional Schroedinger equation for free particle (Gaussian wave-packet), particle in a box, particle in a finite well, linear harmonic oscillator; Reflection and transmission by a step potential and by a rectangular barrier; Particle in a three dimensional box, density of states, free electron theory of metals; Angular momentum; Hydrogen atom; Spin half particles, properties of Pauli spin matrices.

Atomic and Molecular Physics

Stern-Gerlach experiment, electron spin, fine structure of hydrozen atom; L-S coupling, J-J coupling; Spectroscopic notation of atomic states; Zeeman effect; Franck-

Condon principle and applications; Elementary theory of rotational, vibrational and electronic spectra of diatomic molecules; Raman effect and molecular structure; Laser Raman spectroscopy; Importance of neutral hydrogen atom, molecular hydrogen and molecular hydrogen ion in astronomy. Fluorescence and Phosphorescence; Elementary theory and applications of NMR and EPR; Elementary ideas about Lamb shift and its significance.

Nuclear and Particle Physics

- Basic nuclear properties-size, binding energy, angular momentum, parity, magnetic moment; Semi-empirical mass formula and applications. Mass parabolas; Ground state of a deuteron, magnetic moment and non-central forces; Meson theory of nuclear forces; Salient features of nuclear forces; Shell model of the nucleus - success and limitations; Violation of parity in beta decay; Gamma decay and internal conversion; Elementary ideas about Mossbauer spectroscopy; Q-value of nuclear reactions; Nuclear fission and fusion, energy production in stars. Nuclear reactors.
- Classification of elementary particles and their interactions; Conservation laws; Quark structure of hadrons: Field quanta of electroweak and strong interactions; Elementary ideas about unification of forces; Physics of neutrinos.

Solid State Physics, Devices and Electronics

- Crystalline and amorphous structure of matter; Different crystal systems, space groups; Methods of determination of crystal structure; X-ray diffraction, scanning and transmission electron microscopies; Band theory of solids—conductors, insulators and semi-conductors; Thermal properties of solids, specific heat, Debye theory; Magnetism: dia, para and ferromagnetism; Elements of super-conductivity, Meissner effect, Josephson junctions and applications; Elementary ideas about high temperature super-conductivity.
- Intrinsic and extrinsic semi-conductors- p-n-p and n-p-n transistors; Amplifiers and oscillators. Op-amps; FET, JFET and MOSFET; Digital electronics-Boolean identities, De Morgan's laws, Logic gates and truth tables. Simple logic circuits; Thermistors, solar cells; Fundamentals of microprocessors and digital computers.

POLITICAL SCIENCE & INTERNATIONAL RELATIONS

Paper- I

Political Theory and Indian Politics

- **Political Theory:** meaning and approaches.
- **Theories of state:** Liberal, Neo-liberal, Marxist, Pluiralist, post-colonial and Feminist.
- **Justice:** Conceptions of justice with special reference to Rawl's theory of justice and its communitarian critiques.
- **Equality:** Social, political and economic; relationship between equality and freedom; Affirmative action.
- **Rights:** Meaning and theories; different kinds of rights; Concept of Human Rights.
- **Democracy:** Classical and contemporary theories; different models of democracy — representative, participatory and deliberative.
- **Concept of power:** hegemony, ideology and legitimacy.
- **Political Ideologies:** Liberalism, Socialism, Marxism, Fascism, Gandhism and Feminism.
- **Indian Political Thought:** *Dharamshastra, Arthashastra* and Buddhist Traditions; Sir Syed Ahmed Khan, Sri Aurobindo, M. K. Gandhi, B. R. Ambedkar, M. N. Roy.
- **Western Political Thought:** Plato, Aristotle, Machiavelli, Hobbes, Locke, John S. Mill, Marx, Gramsci, Hannah Arendt.

Indian Government and Politics

- **Indian Nationalism:**
  - Political Strategies of India's Freedom Struggle: Constitutionalism to mass Satyagraha, Non-cooperation, Civil Disobedience; Militant and Revolutionary Movements, Peasant and Workers Movements.
  - Perspectives on Indian National Movement; Liberal, Socialist and Marxist; Radical Humanist and Dalit.
- **Making of the Indian Constitution:** Legacies of the British rule; different social and political perspectives.

- **Salient Features of the Indian Constitution:** The Preamble, Fundamental Rights and Duties, Directive Principles; Parliamentary System and Amendment Procedures; Judicial Review and Basic Structure doctrine.
  - Principal Organs of the Union Government: Envisaged role and actual working of the Executive, Legislature and Supreme Court.
  - Principal Organs of the State Government: Envisaged role and actual working of the Executive, Legislature and High Courts.
- **Grassroots Democracy:** Panchayati Raj and Municipal Government; Significance of 73rd and 74th Amendments; Grassroot movements.
- **Statutory Institutions/Commissions:** Election Commission, Comptroller and Auditor General, Finance Commission, Union Public Service Commission, National Commission for Scheduled Castes, National Commission for Scheduled Tribes, National Commission for Women; National Human Rights Commission, National Commission for Minorities, National Backward Classes Commission.
- **Federalism:** Constitutional provisions; changing nature of centre-state relations; integrationist tendencies and regional aspirations; inter-state disputes.
- **Planning and Economic development:** Nehruvian and Gandhian perspectives; Role of planning and public sector; Green Revolution, land reforms and agrarian relations; liberalization and economic reforms.
- Caste, Religion and Ethnicity in Indian Politics.
- **Party System:** National and regional political parties, ideological and social bases of parties; Patterns of coalition politics; Pressure groups, trends in electoral behaviour; changing socio-economic profile of Legislators.
- **Social Movement:** Civil liberties and human rights movements; women's movements; environmentalist movements.

Paper-II

Comparative Politics and International Relations

Comparative Political Analysis and International Politics:

- Comparative Politics: Nature and major approaches; Political economy and political sociology perspectives; Limitations of the comparative method.
- State in Comparative Perspective: Characteristics and changing nature of the State in capitalist and socialist economies, and advanced industrial and developing societies.

- Politics of Representation and Participation: Political parties, pressure groups and social movements in advanced industrial and developing societies.
- Globalisation: Responses from developed and developing societies.
- Approaches to the Study of International Relations: Idealist, Realist, Marxist, Functionalist and Systems theory.
- Key Concepts in International Relations: National interest, security and power; Balance of power and deterrence; Transational actors and collective security; World capitalist economy and globalisation.
- **Changing International Political Order:**
  - Rise of super powers; Strategic and ideological Bipolarity, arms race and cold war; Nuclear threat;
  - Non-aligned Movement: Aims and achievements.
  - Collapse of the Soviet Union; Unipolarity and American hegemony; Relevance of non-alignment in the contemporary world.
- Evolution of the International Economic System: From Brettonwoods to WTO; Socialist economies and the CMEA (Council for Mutual Economic Assistance); Third World demand for new international economic order; Globalisation of the world economy.
- United Nations: Envisaged role and actual record; Specialized UN agencies—aims and functioning; need for UN reforms.
- Regionalisation of World Politics: EU, ASEAN, APEC, AARC, NAFTA.
- Contemporary Global Concerns: Democracy, human rights, environment, gender justice terrorism, nuclear proliferation.

India and the World

- Indian Foreign Policy: Determinants of foreign policy; the institutions of policy-making; Continuity and change.
- India's Contribution to the Non-Alignment Movement Different phases; Current role.
- **India and South Asia:**
  - Regional Co-operation: SAARC-past performance and future prospects.
  - South Asia as a Free Trade Area.
  - India's "Look East" policy.

  - Impediments to regional co-operation: River water disputes; illegal cross border migration; Ethnic conflicts and insurgencies; Border disputes.

- India and the Global South: Relations with Africa and Latin America; Leadership role in the demand for NIEO and WTO negotiations.
- India and the Global Centres of Power: USA, EU, Japan, China and Russia.
- India and the UN System: Role in UN Peace-keeping; Demand for Permanent Seat in the Security Council.
- India and the Nuclear Question: Changing perceptions and policy.
- Recent developments in Indian Foreign Policy: India's position on the recent crises in Afghanistan, Iraq and West Asia, growing relations with US and Isreal; Vision of a new world order.

PSYCHOLOGY

Paper-I

Foundations of Psychology

- **Introduction:** Definition of Psychology; Historical antecedents of Psychology and trends in the 21st centrury; Psychology and scientific methods; Psychology in relation to other social sciences and natural sciences; Application of Psychology to societal problems.
- **Methods of Psychology:** Types of research: Descriptive, evaluative, diagnostic and prognostic; Methods of Research: Survey, observation, case-study and experiments; Characteristics of experimental design and non-experimental designs; quasi-experimental designs; Focussed group discussions, brain storming, grounded theory approach.
- **Research methods:** Major steps in psychological research (problem statement, hypothesis formulation, research design, sampling, tools of data collection, analysis and interpretation and report writing); Fundamental versus applied research; Methods of data collection (interview, observation, questionnaire and case study). Research Designs (Ex-post facto and experimental). Application of statistical techniques (t-test, two-way ANOVA, correlation and regression and factor analysis) item response theory.
- **Development of Human Behaviour:** Growth and development; Principles of development, Role of genetic and environmental factors in determining human behaviour; Influence of cultural factors in socialization; Life span development—Characteristics, development tasks, promoting psychological well-being across major stages of the life span.
- **Sensation, Attention and Perception:** Sensation: concepts of threshold; absolute and difference thresholds, signal-detection and vigilance; Factors influencing attention including set and characteristics of stimulus; Definition and concept of perception, biological factors in perception; Perceptual organization-influence of past experiences, perceptual defence-factor influencing space and depth perception, size estimation and perceptual readiness; The plasticity of perception; Extrasensory perception; Culture and perception, Subliminal perception.
- **Learning:** Concepts and theories of learning (Behaviourists, Gestaltalist and Information processing models). The processes of extinction, discrimination and generalisation. Programmed learning, probability learning, self instructional learning, concepts, types and the schedules of reinforcement, escape, avoidance and punishment, modelling and social learning.

- **Memory:** Encoding and remembering; Shot-term memory, Long-term memory, Sensory memory, Iconic memory, Echoic memory: The Multistore model, levels of processing; Organization and Mnemonic techniques to improve memory; Theories of forgetting: decay, interference and retrieval failure: Metamemory; Amnesia: Anterograde and retrograde.
- **Thinking and Problem Solving:** Piaget's theory of cognitive development; Concept formation processes; Information processing, Reasoning and problem solving, Facilitating and hindering factors in problem solving, Methods of problem solving: Creative thinking and fostering creativity; Factors influencing decision making and judgement; Recent trends.
- **Motivation and Emotion:** Psychological and physiological basis of motivation and emotion; Measurement of motivation and emotion; Effects of motivation and emotion on behaviour; Extrinsic and intrinsic motivation; Factors influencing intrinsic motivation; Emotional competence and the related issues.
- **Intelligence and Aptitude:** Concept of intelligence and aptitude, Nature and theories of intelligence-Spearman, Thurstone, Gulford Vernon, Sternberg and J.P. Das; Emotional Intelligence, Social intelligence, measurement of intelligence and aptitudes, concept of I Q deviation I Q, constancy of I Q; Measurement of multiple intelligence; Fluid intelligence and crystallized intelligence.
- **Personality:** Definition and concept of personality; Theories of personality (psychoanalytical, socio-cultural, interpersonal, developmental, humanistic, behaviouristic, trait and type approaches); Measurement of personality (projective tests, pencil-paper test); The Indian approach to personality; Training for personality development; Latest approaches like big 5 factor theory; The notion of self in different traditions.
- **Attitudes, Values and Interests:** Definitions of attitudes, values and interests; Components of attitudes; Formation and maintenance of attitudes. Measurement of attitudes, values and interests. Theories of attitude changes, strategies for fostering values. Formation of stereotypes and prejudices; Changing other's behaviour, Theories of attribution; Recent trends.
- **Language and Communication:** Human language—Properties, structure and linguistic hierarchy, Language acquisition—predispotion, critical period hypothesis, Theories of Language development—Skinner and Chomsky; Process and types of communication—effective commu-nication training.
- **Issues and Perspectives in Modern Contemporary Psychology:** Computer application in the psychological laboratory and psychological testing; Artificial intelligence; Psychocybernetics; Study of consciousnessleep-wak schedules; dreams, stimulus deprivation, meditation, hypnotic/drug induced states; Extrasensory perception; Intersensory perception; Simulation studies.

Paper-II

Psychology: Issues and applications

- **Psychological Measurement of Individual Differences**
  - The nature of individual differences. Characteristics and construction of standardized psychological tests. Types of psychological tests. Use, misuse and limitation of psychological tests. Ethical issues in the use of psychological tests.
- **Psychological well being and Mental Disorders**
  - Concept of health-ill health positive health, well being casual factores in Mental disorders (Anxiety disorders, mood disorders; schizophrenia and delusional disorders; personality disorders, substance abuse disorders). Factors influencing positive health, well being; lifestyle and quality of life; Happiness disposition.
- **Therapeutic Approaches**
  - Psychodynamic therapies. Behaviour therapies. Client centered therapy. Cognitive therapies. Indigenous therapies (Yoga, Meditation). Biofeedback therapy. Prevention and rehabilitation of the mentally ill; Fostering mental health.
- **Work Psychology and Organisational Behaviour**
  - Personnel selection and training. Use of Psychological tests in the industry. Training and human resource development. Theories of work motivation. Herzberg, Maslow, Adam Equity theory, Porter and Lawler, Vroom; Leadership and participatory management; Advertising and marketing; Stress and its management; Ergonomics; consumer psychology; Managerial effectiveness; Transformational leadersip; Senitivity training; Power and politics in organizations.
- **Application of Psychology to Educational Field**
  - Psychological principles underlying effective teaching-learning process. Learning styles. Gifted, retarded, learning disabled and their training. Training for improving memory and better academic achievement. Personality development and value education. Educational, vocational guidance and Career counselling. Use of Psychological tests in educational institutions; Effective strategies in guidance programmes.
- **Community Psychology**
  - Definition and concept of Community Psychology. Use of small groups in social action. Arousing Community consciousness and action for handling

social problems. Group decision making and leadership for social change. Effective strategies for social change.

- **Rehabilitation Psychology**
  - Primary, secondary and tertiary prevention programmes—role of psychologists. Organising of services for rehabilitation of physically, mentally and socially challenged persons including old persons. Rehabilitation of persons suffering from substance abuse, juvenile delinquency, criminal behaviours. Rehabilitation of victims of violence. Rehabilitation of HIV/AIDS victims, the role of social agencies.
- **Application of Psychology to disadvantaged groups**
  - The concepts of disadvantaged, deprivation social, physical, cultural and economic consequences of disadvantaged and deprived groups. Educating and motivating the disadvantaged towards development; Relative and prolonged deprivation.
- **Psychological problem of social integration**
  - The concept of social integration. The problem of caste, class, religion and language conflicts and prejudice. Nature and manifestation of prejudice between the ingroup and outgroup. Casual factors of such conflicts and prejudices. Psychological strategies for handling the conflicts and prejudices. Measures to achieve social integration.
- **Application of Psychology in Information Technology and Mass Media**
  - The present scenario of information technology and the mass media boom and the role of psychologists. Selection and training of Psychology professionals to work in the field of IT and mass media. Distance learning through IT and mass media. Entrepreneurship through e-commerce.
  - Multilevel marketing. Impact of TV and fostering value through IT and mass media. Psychological consequences of recent developments in Information Technology.
- **Psychology and Economic development**
  - Achievement motivation and economic development. Characteristics of entrepreneurial behaviour. Motivating and Training people for entrepreneurship and economic development; Consumer rights and consumer awareness, Government policies for promotion of entrepreneurship among youth including women entreprenures.
- **Application of Psychology to environment and related fields**
  - Environmental Psychology effects of noise, pollution and crowding. Population Psychology: Psychological consequence of population explosion

and high population density. Motivating for small family norms. Impact of rapid scientific and technological growth on degradation of environment.

- **Application of psychology in other fields**
  - **Military Psychology**
    - Devising psycological tests for defence personnel for use in selection, Training, counseling; training psychologists to work , with defence personnel in promoting positive health; Human engineering in defence.
  - **Sports Psychology**
    - Psychological interventions in improving performance of athletes and sports. Persons participating in Individual and Team Games.
  - Media influences on pro and anti-social behaviour.
  - Psychology of Terrorism.
- **Psychology of Gender:**
  - Issues of discrimination, Management of diversity; Glass ceiling effect, Self-fulfilling prophesy, Women and Indian society.

PUBLIC ADMINISTRATION

Paper-I

Administration Theory

- **Introduction:**
  - Meaning, scope and significance of Public Administration, Wilson's vision of Public Administration, Evolution of the discipline and its present status. New Public Administration, Public Choice approach; Challenges of liberalization, Privatisation, Globalisation; Good Governance: concept and application; New Public Management.
- **Administrative Thought:**
  - Scientific Management and Scientific Management movement; Classical Theory; Weber's bureaucratic model its critique and post-Weberian Developments; Dynamic Administration (Mary Parker Follett); Human Relations School (Elton Mayo and others); Functions of the Executive (C.I. Barnard); Simon's decision-making theory; Participative Management (R. Likert, C. Argyris, D. McGregor.)
- **Administrative Behaviour:**
  - Process and techniques of decision-making; Communication; Morale; Motivation Theories content, process and contemporary; Theories of Leadership: Traditional and Modem:
- **Organisations**
  - Theories systems, contingency; Structure and forms: Ministries and Departments, Corporations, Companies; Boards and Commissions; Ad hoc, and advisory bodies; Headquarters and Field relationships; Regulatory Authorities; Public Private Partnerships.
- **Accountability and Control:**
  - Concepts of accountability and control, Legislative, Executive and judicial control over administration; Citizen and Administration; Role of media, interest groups, voluntary organizations; Civil society; Citizen's Charters; Right to Information; Social audit.
- **Administrative Law:**
  - Meaning, scope and significance; Dicey on Administrative law; Delegated legislation; Administrative Tribunals.

- **Comparative Public Administration**
  - Historical and sociological factors affecting administrative systems; Administration and politics in different countries; Current status of Comparative Public Administration; Ecology and administration; Riggsian models and their critique.
- **Development Dynamics**
  - Concept of development; Changing profile of development administration; 'Anti-development thesis'; Bureaucracy and development; Strong state versus the market debate; Impact of liberalisation on administration in developing countries; Women and development the self-help group movement.
- **Personnel Administration**
  - Importance of human resource development; Recruitment, training, career advancement, position classification, discipline, performance appraisal, promotion, pray and service conditions; employer-employee relations, grievance redressal mechanism; Code of conduct; Administrative ethics.
- **Public Policy**
  - Models of policy-making and their critique; Processes of conceptualisation, planning, implementation, monitoring, evaluation and review and their limitations; State theories and public policy formulation.
- **Techniques of Adminstrative Improvement**
  - Organisation and methods, Work study and work management; e-governance and information technology; Management aid tools like network analysis, MIS, PERT, CPM.
    - **Financial Administration**
  - Monetary and fiscal policies: Public borrowings and public debt Budgets types and forms; Budgetary process; Financial accountability; Accounts and audit.

Paper-II

Indian Administration

- **Evolution of Indian Administration**
  - Kautilya Arthashastra; Mughal administration; Legacy of British rule in politics and administration Indianization of Public services, revenue administration, district Administration, local self Government..

- **Philosophical and Constitutional framework of Government**
  - Salient features and value premises; Constitutionalism; Political culture; Bureaucracy and democracy; Bureaucracy and development.
- **Public Sector Undertakings**
  - Public sector in modern India; Forms of Public Sector Undertakings; Problems of autonomy, accountability and control; Impact of liberalization and privatization.
- **Union Government and Administration**
  - Executive, Parliament, Judiciary-structure, functions, work processes; Recent trends; Intra-governmental relations; Cabinet Secretariat; Prime Minister's Office; Central Secretariat; Ministries and Departments; Boards; Commissions;
  - Attached offices; Field organizations.
- **Plans and Priorities**
  - Machinery of planning; Role, composition and functions of the Planning Commission and the National Development Council; 'Indicative' planning; Process of plan formulation at Union and State levels; Constitutional Amendments (1992) and decentralized planning for economic development and social justice.
- **State Government and Administration**
  - Union-State administrative, legislative and financial relations; Role of the Finance Commission; Governor; Chief Minister; Council of Ministers; Chief Secretary; State Secretariat; Directorates.
- **District Administration since Independence**
  - Changing role of the Collector; Union-State-local relations; Imperatives of development management and law and order administration; District administration and democratic decentralization
- **Civil Services**
  - Constitutional position; Structure, recruitment, training and capacity building; Good governance initiatives; Code of conduct and discipline; Staff associations; Political rights; Grievance redressal mechanism; Civil service neutrality; Civil service activism.
- **Financial Management**
  - Budget as a political instrument, Parliamentary control of public expenditure; Role of finance ministry in monetary and fiscal area; Accounting techniques;

Audit; Role of Controller General of Accounts and Comptroller and Auditor General of India.

- **Administrative Reforms since Independence**
  - Major concerns; Important Committees and Commissions; Reforms in financial management and human resource development; Problems of implementation.
- **Rural Development**
  - Institutions and agencies since Independence; Rural development programmes: foci and strategies; Decentralization and Panchayati Raj; 73rd Constitutional amendment.
- **Urban Local Government**
  - Municipal governance: main features, structures, finance and problem areas; 74th Constitutional Amendment; Global-local debate; New localism; Development dynamics, politics and administration with special reference to city management.
- **Law and Order Administration:**
  - British legacy; National Police Commission; Investigative agencies; Role of Central and State Agencies including para military forces in maintenance of law and order and countering insurgency and terrorism; Criminalisation of politics and administration; Police-public relations; Reforms in Police.
- **Significant issues in Indian Administration**
  - Values in public service; Regulatory Commissions; National Human Rights Commission; Problems of administration in coalition regimes; Citizen administration interface; Corruption and administration; Disaster management.

SOCIOLOGY

Paper– I

Fundamentals of Sociology

- **Sociology - The Discipline**
  - Modernity and social changes in Europe and emergence of Sociology.
  - Scope of the subject and comparison with other social sciences.
  - Sociology and common sense.
- **Sociology as Science**
  - Science, scientific method and critique.
  - Major theoretical strands of research methodology.
  - Positivism and its critique.
  - Fact value and objectivity.
  - Non-positivist methodologies.
- **Research Methods and Analysis**
  - Qualitative and quantitative methods.
  - Techniques of data collection.
  - Variables, sampling, hypothesis, reliability and validity.
- **Sociological Thinkers**
  - Karl Marx - Historical materialism, mode of production, alienation, class struggle.
  - Emile Durkhteim Division of labour, social fact, suicide, religion and society.
  - Max Weber - Social action, ideal types, authority, bureaucracy, protestant ethic and the spirit of capitalism.
  - Talcolt Parsons - Social system, pattern variables.
  - Robert K. Merton - Latent and manifest functions, conformity and deviance, reference groups.
  - Mead - Self and identity.
- **Stratification and Mobility**
  - Concepts - equality, inequality, hierarchy, exclusion, poverty and deprivation.

- Theories of social stratification - Structural func tionalist theory, Marxist theory, Weberian theory.
- Dimensions - Social stratification of class, status groups, gender, ethnicity and race.
- Social mobility - open and closed systems, types of mobility, sources and causes of mobility.

- **Works and Economic Life**
  - Social organization of work in different types of society - slave society, feudal society, industrial capitalist society.
  - Formal and informal organization of work.
  - Labour and society.
- **Politics and Society**
  - Sociological theories of power.
  - Power elite, bureaucracy, pressure groups and political parties.
  - Nation, state, citizenship, democracy, civil society, ideology.
  - Protest, agitation, social movements, collective action, revolution.
- **Religion and Society**
  - Sociological theories of religion.
  - Types of religious practices: animism, monism, pluralism, sects, cults.
  - Religion in modern society: religion and science, secularization, religious revivalism, fundamen talism.
- **Systems of Kinship**
  - Family, household, marriage.
  - Types and forms of family.
  - Lineage and descent.
  - Patriarchy and sexual division of labour.
  - Contem porary trends.
- **Social Change in Modern Society**
  - Sociological theories of social change.
  - Development and dependency.
  - Agents of social change.
  - Education and social change.
  - Science, technology and social change.

Paper–II

Indian Society: Structure and Change

- **Introducing Indian Society:**
  - **Perspectives on the Study of Indian Society:**
    - Indology (G.S. Ghure).
    - Structural functionalism (M. N. Srinivas).
    - Marxist sociology (A. R. Desai).
  - **Impact of colonial rule on Indian society:**
    - Social background of Indian nationalism.
    - Modernization of Indian tradition.
    - Protests and movements during the colonial period.
    - Social reforms.
- **Social Structure:**
  - Rural and Agrarian Social Structure:
    - The idea of Indian village and village studies.
    - Agrarian social structure— evolution of land tenure system, land reforms.
  - **Caste System:**
    - Perspectives on the study of caste systems: G. S. Ghurye, M. N. Srinivas, Louis Dumont, Andre Beteille.
    - Features of caste system.
    - Untouchability-forms and perspectives
  - **Tribal Communities in India:**
    - Definitional problems.
    - Geographical spread.
    - Colonial policies and tribes.
    - Issues of integration and autonomy.
  - **Social Classes in India:**
    - Agrarian class structure.
    - Industrial class structure.
    - Middle classes in India.
  - **Systems of Kinship in India:**
    - Lineage and descent in India.

- Types of kinship systems.
- Family and marriage in India.
- Household dimensions of the family.
- Patriarchy, entitlements and sexual division oflabour.

- **Religion and Society:**
  - Religious communities in India.
  - Problems of religious minorities.

- **Social Changes in India:**
  - **Visions of Social Change in India:**
    - Idea of development planning and mixed economy.
    - Constitution, law and social change.
    - Education and social change.
  - **Rural and Agrarian Transformation in India:**
    - Programmes of rural development, Community Development Programme, cooperatives, poverty alleviation schemes.
    - Green revolution and social change.
    - Changing modes of production in Indian agriculture.
    - Problems of rural labour, bondage, migration.
  - **Industrialization and Urbanisation in India:**
    - Evolution of modern industry in India.
    - Growth of urban settlements in India.
    - Working class: structure, growth, class mobilization.
    - Informal sector, child labour.
    - Slums and deprivation in urban areas.
  - **Politics and Society:**
    - Nation, democracy and citizenship.
    - Political parties, pressure groups, social and political elite.
    - Regionalism and decentralization of power.
    - Secularization.
  - **Social Movements in Modern India:**
    - Peasants and farmers movements.
    - Women's movement.

- Backward classes & Dalit movements.
- Environmental movements.
- Ethnicity and Identity movements.

- **Population Dynamics:**
  - Population size, growth, composition and distribution.
  - Components of population growth: birth, death, migration.
  - Population Policy and family planning.
  - Emerging issues: ageing, sex ratios, child and infant mortality, reproductive health.
- **Challenges of Social Transformation:**
  - Crisis of development: displacement, environmental problems and sustainability.
  - Poverty, deprivation and inequalities.
  - Violence against women.
  - Caste conflicts.
  - Ethnic conflicts, communalism, religious revivalism.
  - Illiteracy and disparities in education.

STATISTICS

Paper–I

Probability

Sample space and events, probability measure and probability space, random variable as a measurable function. Distribution function of a random variable, discrete and continuous-type random variable, probability mass function, probability density function, vector-valued random variable, marginal and conditional distributions, stochastic independence of events and of random variables, expectation and moments of a random variable, conditional expectation, convergence of a sequence of random variable in distribution, in probability, in path mean and almost everywhere, their criteria and inter-relations, Chebyshev's inequality and Khintchine's weak law of large numbers, strong law of large numbers and Kolmogoroffs theorems, probability generating function, moment generating function, characteristic function, inversion theorem, Linderberg and Levy forms of central limit theorem, standard discrete and continuous probability distributions.

Statistical Inference

- Consistency, unbiasedness, efficiency, sufficiency, completeness, ancillary statistics, factorization theorem, exponential family of distribution and its properties, uniformly minimum variance unbiased (UMVU) estimation, Rao Blackwell and Lehmann-Scheffe theorems, Cramer-Rao inequality for single Parameter. Estimation by methods of moments, maximum likelihood, least squares, minimum chisquare and modified minimum chisquare, properties of maximum likelihood and other estimators, asymptotic efficiency, prior and posterior distributions, loss function, risk function, and minimax estimator. Bayes estimators.
- Non-randomised and randomised tests, critical function, MP tests, Neyman-Pearson lemma, UMP tests, monotone likelihood ratio: similar and unbiased tests, UMPU tests for single paramet likelihood ratio test and its asymptotic distribution. Confidence bounds and its relation with tests.
- Kolmogorov's test for goodness of fit and its consistency, sign test and its optimality. Wilcoxon signedranks test and its consistency, Kolmogorov-Smirnov two sample test, run test, Wilcoxon-Mann-Whitney test and median test, their consistency and asymptotic normality.

- Wald's SPRT and its properties, Oc and ASN functions for tests regarding parameters for Bernoulli, Poisson, normal and exponential distributions. Wald's fundamental identity.

Linear Inference and Multivariate Analysis

Linear statistical models, theory of least squares and analysis of variance, Gauss-Markoff theory, normal equations, least squares estimates and their precision, test of significance and interval estimates based on least squares theory in oneway, two-way and three-way classified data, regression analysis, linear regression, curvilinear regression and orthogonal polynomials, multiple regression, multiple and partial correlations, estimation of variance and covariance components, multivariate normal distribution, Mahalanobis's D2 and Hotelling's T2 statistics and their applications and properties, discriminant analysis, canonical correlations, principal component analysis.

Sampling Theory and Design of Experiments

- An outline of fixed-population and super-population approaches, distinctive features of finite population sampling, propability sampling designs, simple random sampling with and without replacement, stratified random sampling, systematic sampling and its efficacy, cluster sampling, twostage and multi-stage sampling, ratio and regression methods of estimation involving one or more auxiliary variables, two-phase sampling, probability proportional to size sampling with and without replacement, the Hansen-Hurwitz and the HorvitzThompson estimators, non-negative variance estimation with reference to the Horvitz-Thompson estimator, non-sampling errors.
- Fixed effects model (two-way classification) random and mixed effects models (two-way classification with equal observation per cell), CRD, RBD, LSD and their analyses, incomplete block designs, concepts of orthogonality and balance, BIBD, missing plot technique, factorial experiments and 24 and 32, confounding in factorial experiments, split-plot and simple lattice designs, transformation of data Duncan's multiple range test.

Paper–II

Industrial Statistics

- Process and product control, general theory of control charts, different types of control charts for variables and attributes, X, R, s, p, np and charts, cumulative sum chart. Single, double, multiple and sequential sampling plans for attributes,

OC, ASN, AOQ and ATI curves, concepts of producer's and consumer's risks, AQL, LTPD and AOQL, Sampling plans for variables, Use of Dodge-Romin tables.

- Concept of reliability, failure rate and reliability functions, reliability of series and parallel systems and other simple configurations, renewal density and renewal function, Failure models: exponential, Weibull, normal, lognormal. Problems in life testing, censored and truncated experiments for exponential models.

Optimization Techniques

- Different types of models in Operations Research, their construction and general methods of solution, simulation and Monte-Carlo methods formulation of Linear Programming (LP) problem, simple LP model and its graphical solution, the simplex procedure, the two-phase metbod and the M-technique with artificial variables, the duality theory of LP and its economic interpretation, sensitivity analysis, transpotation and assignment problems, rectangular games, two-person zero- sum games, methods of solution (graphical and algebraic).
- Replacement of failing or deteriorating items, group and individual replacement policies, concept of scientific inventory management and analytical structure of inventory problems, simple models with deterministic and stochastic demand with and without lead time, storage models with particular reference to dam type.
- Homogeneous discrete-time Markov chains, transition probability matrix, classification of states and ergodic theorems, homogeneous continuous-time Markov chains, Poisson process, elements of queuing theory, M/MI, M/M/K, G/M/l and M/G/1 queues.
- Solution of statistical problems on computers using wellknown statistical software packages like SPSS.

Quantitative Economics and Official Statistics

- Determination of trend, seasonal and cyclical components, Box-Jenkins method, tests for stationary series, ARIMA models and determination of orders of autoregressive and moving average components, fore-casting.
- Commonly used index numbers - Laspeyre's, Paasche's and Fisher's ideal index numbers, cham-base index number, uses and limitations of index numbers, index number of wholesale prices, consumer price, agricultural production and industrial production, test fot index numbers-proportionality, time-reversal, factor-reversal and circular.

- General linear model, ordinary least square and generalized least squares methods of estimation, problem of multi-collinearity, consequences and solutions of multi-collinearity, autocorrelation and its consequences, heteroscedasticity of disturbances and its testing, test for independence of disturbances concept of structure and model for simultaneous equations, problem of identification-rank and order conditions of identifiability, two-stage least sauare method of estimation.
- Present official statistical system in India relating to population, agriculture, industrial production, trade and prices, methods of collection of official statistics, their reliability and limitations, principal publications containing such statistics, various official agencies responsible for data collection and their main functions.

Demography and Psychometry

- Demographic data from census, registration, NSS other surveys, their limitations. and uses, definition, construction and uses of vital rates and ratios, measures of fertility, reproduction rates, morbidity rate, standardized death rate, complete and abridged life tables, construction of life tables from vital statistics and census returns, uses of life tables, logistic and other population growth curves, fitting a logistic curve, population projection, stable population, quasi-stable population, techniques in estimation of demographic parameters, standard classification by cause of death, health surveys and use of hospital statistics.
- Methods of standardisation of scales and tests, Z-scores, standard scores, T-scores, percentile scores, intelligence quotient and its measurement and uses, validity and reliability of test scores and its determination, use of factor analysis and path analysis in psychometry.

ZOOLOGY

Paper–I

Non-chordata and Chordata

- **Classification and relationship of various phyla up to subclasses:** Acoelomate and Coelomate, Protostomes and Deuterostomes, Bilateria and Radiata; Status of Protista, Parazoa, Onychophora and Hemichordata; Symmetry.
- **Protozoa:** Locomotion, nutrition, reproduction, sex; General features and life history of *Paramaecium, Monocystis. Plasmodium* and *Leishmania.*
- **Porifera:** Skeleton, canal system and reproduction.
- **Cnidaria:** Polymorphism, defensive structures and their mechanism; coral reefs and their formation; metagenesis; general features and life history of *Obelia* and *Aurelia.*
- **Platyhelminthes:** Parasitic adaptation; general features and life history of Fasciola and Taenia and their-Pathogenic symptoms.
- **Nemathelminthes:** General features, life history, parasitic adaptation of Ascaris and*Wuchereria.*
- **Annelida:** Coelom and metamerism; modes of life in polychaetes; general features and life history of Nereis, earthworm and leach.
- **Arthropoda:** Larval forms and parasitism in Crustacea; vision and respiration in arthropods (Prawn, cockroach and scorpion); modification of mouth, parts in insects (cockroach, mosquito, housefly, honey bee and butterfly), metapmor phosis in insect and its hormonal regulation, socialbehaviour ofApis and termites.
- **Molluscs:** Feeding, respiration, locomotion, general features and life history of Lamellidens, Pila and Sepia. Torsion and detorsion in gastropods.
- **Echinodermata:** Feeding, respiration, locomotion, larval forms, general features and life history of *Asterias*.
- **Protochordata:** Origin of chordates; general features and life history of *Branchiostoma* and *Herdmania.*
- **Pisces:** Respiration, locomotion and migration.
- **Amphibia:** Origin of tetrapods, parental care, paedomorphosis.
- Reptilia; Origin of reptiles, skull types, status of *Sphenodon* and crocodiles.
- **Aves:** Origin of birds, flight adaptation, migration.

- **Mammalia:** Origin of mammals, dentition, general features of egg laying mammals, pouchedmammals, aquatic mammals and primates, endocrine glands (pituitary, thyroid, parathyroid, adrenal, pancreas, gonads) and their interrelationships.
- Comparative functional anatomy of various systems of vertebrates. (integument and its derivatives, endoskeleton, locomotory organs, digestive system,. respiratory system, circulatory system including heart and aortic arches, urinogenital system, brain and sense organs (eye and ear).

Ecology

- Biosphere: concept of biosphere; biomes, Biogeochemical cycles, Human induced changes in atmosphere including green house effect, ecological succession, biomes and ecotones, community ecology.
- Concept of ecosystem; structure and function of ecosystem, types of ecosystem, ecological succession, ecological adaptation.
- Population; characteristics, population dynamics, population stabilization.
- Biodiversity and diversity conservation of natural resources.
- Wildlife of India.
- Remote sensing for sustainable development.
- Environmental biodegradation; pollution and its impact on biosphere and its prevention.

Ethology

- Behaviour: Sensory filtering, responsiveness, sign stimuli, learning, and memory, instinct, habituation, conditioning, imprinting.
- Role of hormones in drive; role of pheromones in alarm spreading; crypsis, predator detection, predator tactics, social hierarchies in primates, social organization in insects;
- Orientation, navigation, homing; biological rhythms: biological clock, tidal, seasonal and circadian rhythms.
- Methods of studying animal behaviour including sexual conflict, selfishness, kinship and altruism.

Economic Zoology

- Apiculture, sericulture, lac culture, carp culture, pearl culture, prawn culture, vermiculture.

- Major infectious and communicable diseases (malaria, filaria, tuberculosis, cholera and AIDS) their vectors, pathogens and prevention.
- Cattle and livestock diseases, their pathogen (helminths) and vectors (ticks, mites, Tabanus, Stomoxys).
- Pests of sugar cane (*Pyrilla perpusiella*), oil seed *(Achaeajanata)* and rice *(Sitophilus oryzae)*.
- Transgenic animals.
- Medical biotechnology, human genetic disease and genetic counselling, gene therapy. Forensic biotechnology.

Biostatistics

Designing of experiments; null hypothesis; correlation, regression, distribution and measure of central tendency, chi square, student-test, F-test (one-way & two-way F-test).

Instrumentation methods

- Spectrophotometer, phase contrast and fluorescence microscopy, radioactive tracer, ultra centrifuge, gel . electrophoresis, PCR, ELISA, FISH and chromosome painting.
- Electron microscopy (TEM, SEM).

Paper II

Cell Biology

- Structure and function of cell and its organelles (nucleus, plasma membrane, mitochondria, Golgi bodies, endoplasmic reticulum, ribosomes and lysosomes), cell division (mitosis and meiosis), mitotic spindle and mitotic apparatus, chromosome movement chromosome type ploytene and lambrush, organization of chromatin, heterochromatin, Cell cycle regulation.
- Nucleic acid topology, DNA motif, DNA replication, transcription, RNA processing, translation, protein foldings and transport.

Genetics

- Modern concept of gene, split gene, genetic regulation, genetic, code.
- Sex chromosomes and their evolution, sex determination in *Drosophila* and man.

- Mendel's laws of inheritance, recombination, linkage, multiple alleles, genetics of blood groups, pedigree analysis, hereditary diseases in man.
- Mutations and mutagenesis.
- Recombinant DNA technology, plasmid, cosmid, artificial chromosomes as vectors, transgenics, DNA cloning and whole animal cloning (principles and methods).
- Gene regulation and expression in prokaryotes and eukaryotes.
- Signal molecules, cell death, defects in signaling pathway and consequences.
- RFLP, RAPD and AFLF and application of RFLP in DNA finger-printing, ribozyme technologies, human genome project, genomics and protomics.

Evolution

- Theories of origin of life.
- Theories of evolution; Natural selection, role of mutation in evolution, evolutionary patterns, molecular drive, mimicry, variation, isolation and speciation.
- Evolution of horse, elephant and man using fossil data.
- Hardy-Weinberg Law.
- Continental drift and distribution of animals.

Systematics

Zoological nomenclature, international code, cladistics, molecular taxonomy and biodiversity.

Biochemistry

- Structure and role of carbohydrates, fats, fatty acids, cholesterol, proteins and amino-acids, nucleic acids. Bioenergetics.
- Glycolysis and Krebs cycle, oxidation and reduction, oxidative phosphorylation; energy conservation and release, ATP, cycl cyclic AMP-its structure and role.
- Hormone classification (steroid and peptide hormones), biosynthesis and functions.
- Enzymes: types and mechanisms of action.
- Vitamins and co-enzymes.
- Immunoglobulin and immunity.

Physiology (with special reference to mammals)

- Composition and constituents of blood; blood groups and Rh factor in man; factors and mechanism of coagulation; iron metabolism, acid-base balance, thermo regulation, anticoagulants.
- **Haemoglobin:** Composition, types and role in transport of oxygen and carbon dioxide.
- **Digestion and absorption:** Role of salivary glands, liver, pancreas and intestinal glands.
- **Excretion:** nephron and regulation of urine formation; osmo-regulation and excretory product.
- **Muscles:** Types, mechanism of contraction of skeletal muscles, effects of exercise on muscles.
- **Neuron:** nerve impulse—its conduction and synaptic transmission; neurotransmitters.
- Vision, hearing and olfaction in man.
- Physiology of reproduction puberty and menopause in human.

Developmental Biology

- Gametogenesis; spermatogenesis, composition of semen, *in vitro* and *in vivo* capacitation of mammalian sperm, Oogenesis, totipotency; fertilization, morphogenesis and morphogen; blastogeneis, establishment of body axes formation, fate map, gestulation in frog and chick; genes in development in chick homeotic genes, development of eye and heart, placenta in mammals.
- Cell lineage, cell to cell interaction, Genetic and induced teratogenesis, role of thyroxine in control of metamorphosisin amphibia, paedogenesis and neoteny, cell death, aging.
- Developmental genes in man, *in vitro* fertilization; and embryo transfer; cloning.
- Stem cells: Sources, types and their use in human welfare.
- Biogenetic law.

UPSC CSE PRELIMS 2023 GS PAPER I

UPSC Prelims Paper I - 2023

1. In which one of the following regions was Dhanyakataka, which flourished as a prominent Buddhist centre under the Mahasanghikas, located?

(a) Andhra (b) Gandhara

(c) Kalinga (d) Magadha

2. With reference to ancient India, consider the following statements :

1. The concept of Stupa is Buddhist in origin.
2. Stupa was generally a repository of relics.
3. Stupa was a votive and commemorative structure in Buddhist tradition.

How many of the statements given above are correct?

(a) Only one (b) Only two

(c) All three (d) None

3. Which one of the following explains the practice of 'Vattakirutal' as mentioned in Sangam poems?

(a) Kings employing women bodyguards

(b) Learned persons assembling in royal courts to discuss religious and philosophical matters

(c) Young girls keeping watch over agricultural fields and driving away birds and animals

(d) A king defeated in a battle committing ritual suicide by starving himself to death

4. With reference to ancient South India, Korkai, Poompuhar and Muchiri were well known as

(a) capital cities

(b) ports

(c) centers of iron-and-steel making

(d) shrines of Jain Tirthankaras

5. Consider the following dynasties:

1. Hoysala
2. Gahadavala
3. Kakatiya
4. Yadava

How many of the above dynasties established their kingdoms in early eighth century AD?

(a) Only one (b) Only two
(c) Only three (d) None

6. With reference to ancient Indian History, consider the following pairs:

Literary work		***Author***
1. *Devichandragupta*	:	Bilhana
2. *Hammira-Mahakavya*	:	Nayachandra Suri
3. *Milinda-panha*	:	Nagarjuna
4. *Nitivakyamrita*	:	Somadeva Suri

How many of the above pairs are correctly matched?

(a) Only one (b) Only two
(c) Only three (d) All four

7. "Souls are not only the property of animal and plant life, but also of rocks, running water and many other natural objects not looked on as living by other religious sects." The above statement reflects one of the core beliefs of which one of the following religious sects of ancient India?

(a) Buddhism (b) Jainism
(c) Shaivism (d) Vaishnavism

8. Who among the following rulers of Vijayanagara Empire constructed a large dam across Tungabhadra River and a canal-cum-aqueduct several kilometres long from the river to the capital city?

(a) Devaraya I (b) Mallikarjuna
(c) Vira Vijaya (d) Virupaksha

9. Who among the following rulers of medieval Gujarat surrendered Diu to Portuguese?

(a) Ahmad Shah (b) Mahmud Begarha
(c) Bahadur Shah (d) Muhammad Shah

10. By which one of the following Acts was the Governor General of Bengal designated as the Governor General of India?

(a) The Regulating Act
(b) The Pitt's India Act
(c) The Charter Act of 1793
(d) The Charter Act of 1833

11. In essence, what does 'Due Process of Law' mean?

(a) The principle of natural justice

(b) The procedure established by law

(c) Fair application of law

(d) Equality before law

12. Consider the following statements:

Statement-I: In India, prisons are managed by State Governments with their own rules and regulations for the day-to-day administration of prisons.

Statement-II: In India, prisons are governed by the Prisons Act, 1894 which expressly kept the subject of prisons in the control of Provincial Governments.

Which one of the following is correct in respect of the above statements?

(a) Both Statement-I and Statement-II are correct, and Statement-II is the correct explanation for Statement-I

(b) Both Statement-I and Statement-II are correct, and Statement-II is not the correct explanation for Statement-I

(c) Statement-I is correct, but Statement-II is incorrect

(d) Statement-I is incorrect, but Statement-II is correct

13. Which one of the following statements best reflects the **Chief** purpose of the 'Constitution' of a country?

(a) It determines the objective for the making of necessary laws.

(b) It enables the creation of political offices and a government.

(c) It defines and limits the powers of government.

(d) It secures social justice, social equality and social security.

14. In India, which one of the following Constitutional Amendments was widely believed to be enacted to overcome the judicial interpretations of the Fundamental Rights?

(a) 1st Amendment (b) 42nd Amendment

(c) 44th Amendment (d) 86th Amendment

15. Consider the following organizations/bodies in India:

1. The National Commission for Backward Classes
2. The National Human Rights Commission
3. The National Law Commission
4. The National Consumer Disputes Redressal Commission

How many of the above are constitutional bodies?

(a) Only one (b) Only two

(c) Only three (d) All four

16. Consider the following statements:

1. If the election of the President of India is declared void by the Supreme Court of India, all acts done by him/her in the performance of duties of his/her office of President before the date of decision become invalid.
2. Election for the post of the President of India can be postponed on the ground that some Legislative Assemblies have been dissolved and elections are yet to take place.
3. When a Bill is presented to the President of India, the Constitution prescribes time limits within which he/she has to declare his/her assent.

How many of the above statements are correct?

(a) Only one (b) Only two

(c) All three (d) None

17. With reference to Finance Bill and Money Bill in the Indian Parliament, consider the following statements:

1. When the Lok Sabha transmits Finance Bill to the Rajya Sabha, it can amend or reject the Bill.
2. When the Lok Sabha transmits Money Bill to the Rajya Sabha, it cannot amend or reject the Bill, it can only make recommendations.
3. In the case of disagreement between the Lok Sabha and the Rajya Sabha, there is no joint sitting for Money Bill, but a joint sitting becomes necessary for Finance Bill.

How many of the above statements are correct?

(a) Only one (b) Only two

(c) All three (d) None

18. Consider the following statements :

Once the Central Government notifies an area as a 'Community Reserve'

1. the Chief Wildlife Warden of the State becomes the governing authority of such forest
2. hunting is not allowed in such area
3. people of such area are allowed to collect non-timber forest produce
4. people of such area are allowed traditional agricultural practices

How many of the above statements are correct?

(a) Only one (b) Only two

(c) Only three (d) All four

19. With reference to 'Scheduled Areas' in India, consider the following statements :

1. Within a State, the notification of an area as Scheduled Area takes place through an Order of the President.
2. The largest administrative unit forming the Scheduled Area is the district and the lowest is the cluster of villages in the Block.
3. The Chief Ministers of the concerned States are required to submit annual reports to the Union Home Ministry on the administration of Scheduled Areas in the States.

How many of the above statements are correct?

(a) Only one (b) Only two

(c) All three (d) None

20. Consider the following statements:

Statement-I: The Supreme Court of India has held in some judgements that the reservation policies made under Article 16(4) of the Constitution of India would be limited by Article 335 for maintenance of efficiency of administration.

Statement-II: Article 335 of the Constitution of India defines the term 'efficiency of administration'.

Which one of the following is correct in respect of the above statements?

(a) Both Statement-I and Statement-II are correct and Statement-II is the correct explanation for Statement-I

(b) Both Statement-I and Statement-II are correct and Statement-II is not the correct explanation for Statement-I

(c) Statement-I is correct but Statement-II is incorrect

(d) Statement-I is incorrect but Statement-II is correct

21. Consider the following statements:

Statement-I: India, despite having uranium deposits, depends on coal for most of its electricity production.

Statement-II: Uranium, enriched to the extent of at least 60%, is required for the production of electricity.

Which one of the following is correct in respect of the above statements?

(a) Both Statement-I and Statement-II are correct and Statement-II is the correct explanation for Statement-I

(b) Both Statement-I and Statement-II are correct and Statement-II is not the correct explanation for Statement-I

(c) Statement-I is correct, but Statement-II is incorrect

(d) Statement-I is incorrect, but Statement-II is correct

22. Consider the following statements:

Statement-I: Marsupials are not naturally found in India.

Statement-II: Marsupials can thrive only in montane grasslands with no predators.

Which one of the following is correct in respect of the above statements?

(a) Both Statement-I and Statement-II are correct and Statement-II is the correct explanation for Statement-I

(b) Both Statement-I and Statement-II are correct and Statement-II is not the correct explanation for Statement-I

(c) Statement-I is correct but Statement-II is incorrect

(d) Statement-I is incorrect but Statement-II is correct

23. 'Invasive Species Specialist Group' (that develops Global Invasive Species Database) belongs to which one of the following organizations?

(a) The International Union for Conservation of Nature

(b) The United Nations Environment Programme

(c) The United Nations World Commission for Environment and Development

(d) The Worldwide Fund for Nature

24. Consider the following fauna:

1. Lion-tailed Macaque
2. Malabar Civet
3. Sambar Deer

How many of the above are generally nocturnal or most active after sunset?

(a) Only one (b) Only two

(c) All three (d) None

25. Which of the following organisms perform waggle dance for others of their kin to indicate the direction and the distance to a source of their food?

(a) Butterflies (b) Dragonflies

(c) Honeybees (d) Wasps

26. Consider the following statements:

1. Some mushrooms have medicinal properties.
2. Some mushrooms have psychoactive properties.
3. Some mushrooms have insecticidal properties.
4. Some mushrooms have bioluminescent properties.

How many of the above statements are correct?

(a) Only one (b) Only two
(c) Only three (d) All four

27. Consider the following statements regarding the Indian squirrels:

1. They build nests by making burrows in the ground.
2. They store their food materials like nuts and seeds in the ground.
3. They are omnivorous.

How many of the above statements are correct?

(a) Only one (b) Only two
(c) All three (d) None

28. Consider the following statements:

1. Some microorganisms can grow in environments with temperature above the boiling point of water.
2. Some microorganisms can grow in environments with temperature below the freezing point of water.
3. Some microorganisms can grow in highly acidic environment with a pH below 3.

How many of the above statements are correct?

(a) Only one (b) Only two
(c) All three (d) None

29. Which one of the following makes a tool with a stick to scrape insects from a hole in a tree or a log of wood?

(a) Fishing cat (b) Orangutan
(c) Otter (d) Sloth bear

30. Consider the following:

1. Aerosols 2. Foam agents
3. Fire retardants 4. Lubricants

In the making of how many of the above are hydrofluorocarbons used?

(a) Only one
(b) Only two
(c) Only three
(d) All four

31. Consider the following statements:

1. Jhelum River passes through Wular Lake.
2. Krishna River directly feeds Kolleru Lake.
3. Meandering of Gandak River formed Kanwar Lake.

How many of the statements given above are correct?

(a) Only one
(b) Only two
(c) All three
(d) None

32. Consider the following pairs:

Port		*Well known as*
1. Kamarajar Port	:	First major port in India registered as a company
2. Mundra Port	:	Largest privately owned port in India
3. Visakhapatnam Port	:	Largest container port in India

How many of the above pairs are correctly matched?

(a) Only one pair
(b) Only two pairs
(c) All three pairs
(d) None of the pairs

33. Consider the following trees:

1. Jackfruit (*Artocarpus heterophyllus*)
2. Mahua (*Madhuca indica*)
3. Teak (*Tectona grandis*)

How many of the above are deciduous trees?

(a) Only one
(b) Only two
(c) All three
(d) None

34. Consider the following statements:

1. India has more arable area than China.
2. The proportion of irrigated area is more in India as compared to China.
3. The average productivity per hectare in Indian agriculture is higher than that in China.

How many of the above statements are correct?

(a) Only one
(b) Only two
(c) All three
(d) None

35. Which one of the following is the best example of repeated falls in sea level, giving rise to present-day extensive marshland?

(a) Bhitarkanika Mangroves

(b) Marakkanam Salt Pans

(c) Naupada Swamp

(d) Rann of Kutch

36. Ilmenite and rutile, abundantly available in certain coastal tracts of India, are rich sources of which one of the following?

(a) Aluminium (b) Copper

(c) Iron (d) Titanium

37. About three-fourths of world's cobalt, a metal required for the manufacture of batteries for electric motor vehicles, is produced by

(a) Argentina

(b) Botswana

(c) the Democratic Republic of the Congo

(d) Kazakhstan

38. Which one of the following is a part of the Congo Basin?

(a) Cameroon (b) Nigeria

(c) South Sudan (d) Uganda

39. Consider the following statements:

1. Amarkantak Hills are at confluence of Vindhya and Sahyadri Ranges.
2. Biligirirangan Hills constitute the easternmost part of Satpura Range.
3. Seshachalam Hills constitute the southernmost part of Western Ghats.

How many of the statements given above are correct?

(a) Only one (b) Only two

(c) All three (d) None

40. With reference to India's projects on connectivity, consider the following statements:

1. East-West Corridor under Golden Quadrilateral Project connects Dibrugarh and Surat.
2. Trilateral Highway connects Moreh in Manipur and Chiang Mai in Thailand via Myanmar.
3. Bangladesh-China-India-Myanmar Economic Corridor connects Varanasi in Uttar Pradesh with Kunming in China.

How many of the above statements are correct?

(a) Only one (b) Only two

(c) All three (d) None

41. Consider the following statements:

Statement-I: Interest income from the deposits in Infrastructure Investment Trusts (InvITs) distributed to their investors is exempted from tax, but the dividend is taxable.

Statement-II: InvITs are recognized as borrowers under the 'Securitization and Reconstruction of Financial Assets and Enforcement of Security Interest Act, 2002'.

Which one of the following is correct in respect of the above statements?

(a) Both Statement-I and Statement-II are correct and Statement-II is the correct explanation for Statement-I

(b) Both Statement-I and Statement-II are correct and Statement-II is not the correct explanation for Statement-I

(c) Statement-I is correct but Statement-II is incorrect

(d) Statement-I is incorrect but Statement-II is correct

42. Consider the following statements :

Statement-I: In the post-pandemic recent past, many Central Banks worldwide had carried out interest rate hikes.

Statement-II: Central Banks generally assume that they have the ability to counteract the rising consumer prices via monetary policy means.

Which one of the following is correct in respect of the above statements?

(a) Both Statement-I and Statement-II are correct and Statement-II is the correct explanation for Statement-I

(b) Both Statement-I and Statement-II are correct and Statement-II is not the correct explanation for Statement-I

(c) Statement-I is correct but Statement-II is incorrect

(d) Statement-I is incorrect but Statement-II is correct

43. Consider the following statements:

Statement-I: Carbon markets are likely to be one of the most widespread tools in the fight against climate change.

Statement-II: Carbon markets transfer resources from the private sector to the State.

Which one of the following is correct in respect of the above statements?

(a) Both Statement-I and Statement-II are correct and Statement-II is the correct explanation for Statement-I

(b) Both Statement-I and Statement-II are correct and Statement-II is not the correct explanation for Statement-I

(c) Statement-I is correct but Statement-II is incorrect

(d) Statement-I is incorrect but Statement-II is correct

44. Which one of the following activities of the Reserve Bank of India is considered to be part of 'sterilization'?

(a) Conducting 'Open Market Operations'

(b) Oversight of settlement and payment systems

(c) Debt and cash management for the Central and State Governments

(d) Regulating the functions of Non-banking Financial Institutions

45. Consider the following markets:

1. Government Bond Market
2. Call Money Market
3. Treasury Bill Market
4. Stock Market

How many of the above are included in capital markets?

(a) Only one (b) Only two

(c) Only three (d) All four

46. Which one of the following best describes the concept of 'Small Farmer Large Field'?

(a) Resettlement of a large number of people, uprooted from their countries due to war, by giving them a large cultivable land which they cultivate collectively and share the produce

(b) Many marginal farmers in an area organize themselves into groups and synchronize and harmonize selected agricultural operations

(c) Many marginal farmers in an area together make a contract with a corporate body and surrender their land to the corporate body for a fixed term for which the corporate body makes a payment of agreed amount to the farmers

(d) A company extends loans, technical knowledge and material inputs to a number of small farmers in an area so that they produce the agricultural commodity required by the company for its manufacturing process and commercial production

47. Consider the following statements:

1. The Government of India provides Minimum Support Price for niger (*Guizotia abyssinica*) seeds.
2. Niger is cultivated as a Kharif crop.
3. Some tribal people in India use niger seed oil for cooking.

How many of the above statements are correct?

(a) Only one (b) Only two
(c) All three (d) None

48. Consider the investments in the following assets:

1. Brand recognition
2. Inventory
3. Intellectual property
4. Mailing list of clients

How many of the above are considered intangible investments?

(a) Only one (b) Only two
(c) Only three (d) All four

49. Consider the following:

1. Demographic performance 2. Forest and ecology
3. Governance reforms 4. Stable government
5. Tax and fiscal efforts

For the horizontal tax devolution, the Fifteenth Finance Commission used how many of the above as criteria other than population area and income distance?

(a) Only two (b) Only three
(c) Only four (d) All five

50. Consider the following infrastructure sectors:

1. Affordable housing 2. Mass rapid transport
3. Health care 4. Renewable energy

On how many of the above does UNOPS Sustainable Investments in Infrastructure and Innovation (S3i) initiative focus for its investments?

(a) Only one (b) Only two
(c) Only three (d) All four

51. With reference to Home Guards, consider the following statements:

1. Home Guards are raised under the Home Guards Act and Rules of the Central Government.

2. The role of the Home Guards is to serve as an auxiliary force to the police in maintenance of internal security.
3. To prevent infiltration on the international border/coastal areas, the Border Wing Home Guards Battalions have been raised in some States.

How many of the above statements are correct?

(a) Only one (b) Only two
(c) All three (d) None

52. With reference to India, consider the following pairs:

Action		The Act under which it is covered
1. Unauthorized wearing of police or military uniforms	:	The Official Secrets Act, 1923
2. Knowingly misleading or otherwise interfering with a police officer or military officer when engaged in their duties	:	The Indian Evidence Act, 1872
3. Celebratory gunfire which can endanger the personal safety of others	:	The Arms (Amendment) Act, 2019

How many of the above pairs are correctly matched?

(a) Only one (b) Only two
(c) All three (d) None

53. Consider the following pairs:

Regions often mentioned in news		*Reason for being in news*
1. North Kivu and Ituri	:	War between Armenia and Azerbaijan
2. Nagorno-Karabakh	:	Insurgency in Mozambique
3. Kherson and Zaporizhzhia	:	Dispute between Israel and Lebanon

How many of the above pairs are correctly matched?

(a) Only one (b) Only two
(c) All three (d) None

54. Consider the following statements:

Statement-I: Israel has established diplomatic relations with some Arab States.

Statement-II: The 'Arab Peace Initiative' mediated by Saudi Arabia was signed by Israel and Arab League.

Which one of the following is correct in respect of the above statements?

(a) Both Statement-I and Statement-II are correct, and Statement-II is the correct explanation for Statement-I

(b) Both Statement-I and Statement-II are correct, and Statement-II is not the correct explanation for Statement-I

(c) Statement-I is correct but Statement-II is incorrect

(d) Statement-I is incorrect but Statement-II is correct

55. Consider the following pairs with regard to sports awards:

	Awards		***Purpose***
1.	Major Dhyan Chand Khel Ratna Award	:	For the most spectacular and outstanding performance over period of last four years
2.	Arjuna Award	:	For the lifetime achievement by sportsperson
3.	Dronacharya Award	:	To honour eminent coaches who have successfully trained sportspersons or teams
4.	Rashtriya Khel Protsahan Puraskar	:	To recognize the contribution made by sportspersons even after their retirement

How many of the above pairs are correctly matched?

(a) Only one (b) Only two

(c) Only three (d) All four

56. Consider the following statements in respect of the 44th Chess Olympiad, 2022:

1. It was the first time that Chess Olympiad was held in India.
2. The official mascot was named 'Thambi'.
3. The trophy for the winning team in the open section is the Vera Menchik Cup.
4. The trophy for the winning team in the women's section is the Hamilton-Russell Cup.

How many of the statements given above are correct?

(a) Only one

(b) Only two

(c) Only three

(d) All four

57. In the recent years Chad, Guinea, Mali and Sudan caught the international attention for which one of the following reasons common to all of them?

(a) Discovery of rich deposits of rare earth elements

(b) Establishment of Chinese military bases

(c) Southward expansion of Sahara Desert

(d) Successful coups

58. Consider the following pairs:

Area of conflict mentioned in news		***Country where it is located***
1. Donbas	:	Syria
2. Kachin	:	Ethiopia
3. Tigray	:	North Yemen

How many of the above pairs are correctly matched?

(a) Only one (b) Only two

(c) All three (d) None

59. Consider the following heavy industries :

1. Fertilizer plants
2. Oil refineries
3. Steel plants

Green hydrogen is expected to play a significant role in decarbonizing how many of the above industries?

(a) Only one (b) Only two

(c) All three (d) None

60. Consider the following statements about G-20 :

1. The G-20 group was originally established as a platform for the Finance Ministers and Central Bank Governors to discuss the international economic and financial issues.
2. Digital public infrastructure is one of India's G-20 priorities.

Which of the statements given above is/are correct?

(a) 1 only

(b) 2 only

(c) Both 1 and 2

(d) Neither 1 nor 2

61. With reference to the Indian History, Alexander Rea, A. H. Longhurst, Robert Sewell, James Burgess and Walter Elliot were associated with

(a) archaeological excavations

(b) establishment of English Press in Colonial India

(c) establishment of Churches in Princely States

(d) construction of railways in Colonial India

62. Consider the following pairs :

	Site		***Well known for***
1.	Besnagar	:	Shaivite cave shrine
2.	Bhaja	:	Buddhist cave shrine
3.	Sittanavasal	:	Jain cave shrine

How many of the above pairs are correctly matched?

(a) Only one

(b) Only two

(c) All three

(d) None

63. Consider the following statements :

Statement-I: 7th August is declared as the National Handloom Day.

Statement-II: It was in 1905 that the Swadeshi Movement was launched on the same day.

Which one of the following is correct in respect of the above statements?

(a) Both Statement-I and Statement-II are correct and Statement-II is the correct explanation for Statement-I

(b) Both Statement-I and Statement-II are correct and Statement-II is not the correct explanation for Statement-I

(c) Statement-I is correct but Statement-II is incorrect

(d) Statement-I is incorrect but Statement-II is correct

64. Consider the following statements in respect of the National Flag of India according to the Flag Code of India, 2002:

Statement-I: One of the standard sizes of the National Flag of India is 600 mm × 400 mm.

Statement-II: The ratio of the length to the height (width) of the Flag shall be 3:2.

Which one of the following is correct in respect of the above statements?

(a) Both Statement-I and Statement-II are correct and Statement-II is the correct explanation for Statement-I

(b) Both Statement-I and Statement-II are correct and Statement-II is not the correct explanation for Statement-I

(c) Statement-I is correct but Statement-II is incorrect

(d) Statement-I is incorrect but Statement-II is correct

65. Consider the following statements in respect of the Constitution Day:

Statement-I: The Constitution Day is celebrated on 26th November every year to promote constitutional values among citizens.

Statement-II: On 26th November, 1949, the Constituent Assembly of India set up a Drafting Committee under the Chairmanship of Dr. B.R. Ambedkar to prepare a Draft Constitution of India.

Which one of the following is correct in respect of the above statements?

(a) Both Statement-I and Statement-II are correct and Statement-II is the correct explanation for Statement-I

(b) Both Statement-I and Statement-II are correct and Statement-II is not the correct explanation for Statement-I

(c) Statement-I is correct but Statement-II is incorrect

(d) Statement-I is incorrect but Statement-II is correct

66. Consider the following statements:

Statement-I: Switzerland in one of the leading exporters of gold in terms of value.

Statement-II: Switzerland has the second largest gold reserves in the world.

Which one of the following is correct in respect of the above statements?

(a) Both Statement-I and Statement-II are correct and Statement-II is the correct explanation for Statement-I

(b) Both Statement-I and Statement-II are correct and Statement-II is not the correct explanation for Statement-I

(c) Statement-I is correct but Statement-II is incorrect

(d) Statement-I is incorrect but Statement-II is correct

67. Consider the following statements:

Statements-I: Recently, the United States of America (USA) and the European Union (EU) have launched the 'Trade and Technology Council'.

Statement-II: The USA and the EU claim that through this they are trying to bring technological progress and physical productivity under their control.

Which one of the following is correct in respect of the above statements?

(a) Both Statement-I and Statement-II are correct, and Statement-II is the correct explanation for Statement-I

(b) Both Statement-I and Statement-II are correct, and Statement-II is not the correct explanation for Statement-I

(c) Statement-I is correct, but Statement-II is incorrect

(d) Statement-I is incorrect, but Statement-II is correct

68. Consider, the following statements:

Statement-I: India accounts for 3.2% of global export of goods.

Statement-II: Many local companies and some foreign companies operating in India have taken advantage of India's 'Production-linked Incentive' scheme.

Which one of the following is correct in respect of the above statements?

(a) Both Statement-I and Statement-II are correct, and Statement-II is the correct explanation for Statement-I

(b) Both Statement-I and Statement-II are correct, and Statement-II is not the correct explanation for Statement-I

(c) Statement-I is correct but Statement-II is incorrect

(d) Statement-I is incorrect but Statement-II is correct

69. Consider the following statements:

The 'Stability and Growth Pact' of the European Union is a treaty that

1. limits the levels of the budgetary deficit of the countries of the European Union
2. makes the countries of the European Union to share their infrastructure facilities
3. enables the countries of the European Union to share their technologies

How many of the above statements are correct?

(a) Only one (b) Only two

(c) All three (d) None

70. Consider the following statements:

1. Recently, all the countries of the United Nations have adopted the first-ever compact for international migration, the 'Global Compact for Safe, Orderly and Regular Migration (GCM)'.
2. The objectives and commitments stated in the GCM are binding on the UN member countries.

3. The GCM addresses internal migration or internally displaced people also in its objectives and commitments.

How many of the above statements are:

(a) Only one (b) Only two

(c) All three (d) None

71. Consider the following countries:

1. Bulgaria
2. Czech Republic
3. Hungary
4. Latvia
5. Lithuania
6. Romania

How many of the above-mentioned countries share a land border with Ukraine?

(a) Only two (b) Only three

(c) Only four (d) Only five

72. With reference to the Earth's atmosphere, which one of the following statements is correct?

(a) The total amount of insolation received at the equator is roughly about 10 times of that received at the poles.

(b) Infrared rays constitute roughly two-thirds of insolation.

(c) Infrared waves are largely absorbed by water vapors that are concentrated in the lower atmosphere.

(d) Infrared waves are a part of visible spectrum of electromagnetic waves of solar radiation.

73. Consider the following statements:

Statement-I: The soil in tropical rain forests is rich in nutrients.

Statement-II: The high temperature and moisture of tropical rain forests cause dead organic matter in the soil to decompose quickly.

Which one of the following is correct in respect of the above statements?

(a) Both Statement-I and Statement-II are correct, and Statement-II is the correct explanation for Statement-I

(b) Both Statement-I and Statement-II are correct, and Statement-II is not the correct explanation for Statement-I

(c) Statement-I is correct but Statement-II is incorrect

(d) Statement-I is incorrect but Statement-II is correct

74. Consider the following statements :

Statement-I: The temperature contrast between continents and oceans is greater during summer than in winter.

Statement-II: The specific heat of water is more than that of land surface.

Which one of the following is correct in respect of the above statements?

(a) Both Statement-I and Statement-II are correct and Statement-II is the correct explanation for Statement-I

(b) Both Statement-I and Statement-II are correct and Statement-II is not the correct explanation for Statement-I

(c) Statement-I is correct but Statement-II is incorrect

(d) Statement-I is incorrect but Statement-II is correct

75. Consider the following statements:

1. In a seismograph, P waves are recorded earlier than S waves.
2. In P waves, the individual particles vibrate to and fro in the direction of wave propagation whereas in S waves, the particles vibrate up and down at right angles to the direction of wave propagation.

Which of the statements given above is/are correct?

(a) 1 only (b) 2 only

(c) Both 1 and 2 (d) Neither 1 nor 2

76. With reference to coal-based thermal power plants in India, consider the following statements:

1. None of them uses seawater.
2. None of them is set up in water-stressed district.
3. None of them is privately owned.

How many of the above statements are correct?

(a) Only one (b) Only two

(c) All three (d) None

77. 'Wolbachia method' is sometimes talked about with reference to which one of the following?

(a) Controlling the viral diseases spread by mosquitoes

(b) Converting crop residues into packing material

(c) Producing biodegradable plastics

(d) Producing biochar from thermo-chemical conversion of biomass

78. Consider the following activities:

1. Spreading finely ground basalt rock on farmlands extensively
2. Increasing the alkalinity of oceans by adding lime
3. Capturing carbon dioxide released by various industries and pumping it into abandoned subterranean mines in the form of carbonated waters

How many of the above activities are often considered and discussed for carbon capture and sequestration?

(a) Only one (b) Only two

(c) All three (d) None

79. 'Aerial metagenomics' best refers to which one of the following situations?

(a) Collecting DNA samples from air in a habitat at one go

(b) Understanding the genetic makeup of avian species of a habitat

(c) Using air-borne devices to collect blood samples from moving animals

(d) Sending drones to inaccessible areas to collect plant and animal samples from land surfaces and water bodies

80. 'Microsatellite DNA' is used in the case of which one of the following?

(a) Studying the evolutionary relationships among various species of fauna

(b) Stimulating 'stem cells' to transform into diverse functional tissues

(c) Promoting clonal propagation of horticultural plants

(d) Assessing the efficacy of drugs by conducting series of drug trials in a population

81. Consider the following statements in relation to Janani Suraksha Yojana:

1. It is a safe motherhood intervention of the State Health Departments.
2. Its objective is to reduce maternal and neonatal mortality among poor pregnant women.
3. It aims to promote institutional delivery among poor pregnant women.
4. Its objective includes providing public health facilities to sick infants up to one year of age.

How many of the statements given above are correct?

(a) Only one (b) Only two

(c) Only three (d) All four

82. Consider the following statements in the context of interventions being undertaken under Anaemia Mukt Bharat Strategy:

1. It provides prophylactic calcium supplementation for pre school children, adolescents and pregnant women.

2. It runs a campaign for delayed cord clamping at the time of childbirth.
3. It provides for periodic deworming to children and adolescents.
4. It addresses non-nutritional causes of anaemia in endemic pockets with special focus on malaria, hemoglobinopathies and fluorosis.

How many of the statements given above are correct?

(a) Only one (b) Only two
(c) Only three (d) All four

83. Consider the following statements:

1. Carbon fibres are used in the manufacture of components used in automobiles and aircrafts.
2. Carbon fibres once used cannot be recycled.

Which of the statements given above is/are correct?

(a) 1 only
(b) 2 only
(c) Both 1 and 2
(d) Neither 1 nor 2

84. Consider the following actions:

1. Detection of car crash/collision which results in the deployment of airbags almost instantaneously
2. Detection of accidental free fall of a laptop towards the ground which results in the immediate turning off of the hard drive
3. Detection of the tilt of smartphone which results in the rotation of display between portrait and landscape mode

In how many of the above actions is the function of accelerometer required?

(a) Only one (b) Only two
(c) All three (d) None

85. With reference to the role of biofilters in Recirculating Aquaculture System, consider the following statements:

1. Biofilters provide waste treatment by removing uneaten fish feed.
2. Biofilters convert ammonia present in fish waste to nitrate.
3. Biofilters increase phosphorus as nutrient for fish in water.

How many of the statements given above are correct?

(a) Only one (b) Only two
(c) All three (d) None

86. Consider the following pairs:

Objects in space		**Description**
1. Cepheids	:	Giant clouds of dust and gas in space
2. Nebulae	:	Stars which brighten and dim periodically
3. Pulsars	:	Neutron stars that are formed when massive stars run out of fuel and collapse

How many of the above pairs are correctly matched?

(a) Only one (b) Only two

(c) All three (d) None

87. Which one of the following countries has its own Satellite Navigation System?

(a) Australia (b) Canada

(c) Israel (d) Japan

88. Consider the following statements:

1. Ballistic missiles are jet-propelled at subsonic speeds throughout their flights, while cruise missiles are rocket-powered only in the initial phase of flight.
2. Agni-V is a medium-range supersonic cruise missile, while BrahMos is a solid-fuelled intercontinental ballistic missile.

Which of the statements given above is/are correct?

(a) 1 only (b) 2 only

(c) Both 1 and 2 (d) Neither 1 nor 2

89. Consider the following statements regarding mercury pollution:

1. Gold mining activity is a source of mercury pollution in the world.
2. Coal-based thermal power plants cause mercury pollution.
3. There is no known safe level of exposure to mercury.

How many of the above statements are correct?

(a) Only one (b) Only two

(c) All three (d) None

90. With reference to green hydrogen, consider the following statements:

1. It can be used directly as a fuel for internal combustion.
2. It can be blended with natural gas and used as fuel for heat or power generation.
3. It can be used in the hydrogen fuel cell to run vehicles.

How many of the above statements are correct?

(a) Only one (b) Only two

(c) All three (d) None

91. Consider the following statements with reference to India:

1. According to the 'Micro, Small and Medium Enterprises Development (MSMED) Act, 2006', the 'medium enterprises' are those with investments in plant and machinery between Rs. 15 crore and Rs. 25 crore.
2. All bank loans to the Micro, Small and Medium Enterprises qualify under the priority sector.

Which of the statements given above is/are correct?

(a) 1 only (b) 2 only
(c) Both 1 and 2 (d) Neither 1 nor 2

92. With reference to Central Bank digital currencies, consider the following statements:

1. It is possible to make payments in a digital currency without using US dollar or SWIFT system.
2. A digital currency can be distributed with a condition programmed into it such as a timeframe for spending it.

Which of the statements given above is/are correct?

(a) 1 only (b) 2 only
(c) Both 1 and 2 (d) Neither 1 nor 2

93. In the context of finance, the term 'beta' refers to

(a) the process of simultaneous buying and selling of an asset from different platforms
(b) an investment strategy of a portfolio manager to balance risk versus reward
(c) a type of systemic risk that arises where perfect hedging is not possible
(d) a numeric value that measures the fluctuations of a stock to changes in the overall stock market.

94. Consider the following statements:

1. The Self-Help Group (SHG) programme was originally initiated by the State Bank of India by providing microcredit to the financially deprived.
2. In an SHG, all members of a group take responsibility for a loan that an individual member takes.
3. The Regional Rural Banks and Scheduled Commercial Banks support SHGs.

How many of the above statements are correct?

(a) Only one (b) Only two
(c) All three (d) None

95. Consider the following statements:

Statement-I: India's public sector health care system largely focuses on curative care with limited preventive, promotive and rehabilitative care.

Statement-II: Under India's decentralized approach to health care delivery, the States are primarily responsible for organizing health services.

Which one of the following is correct in respect of the above statements?

(a) Both Statement-I and Statement-II are correct, and Statement-II is the correct explanation for Statement-I

(b) Both Statement-I and Statement-II are correct, and Statement-II is not the correct explanation for Statement-I

(c) Statement-I is correct but Statement-II is incorrect

(d) Statement-I is incorrect but Statement-II is correct

96. Consider the following statements:

Statement-I: According to the United Nations 'World Water Development Report, 2022', India extracts more than a quarter of the world's groundwater withdrawal each year.

Statement-II: India needs to extract more than a quarter of the world's groundwater each year to satisfy the drinking water and sanitation needs of almost 18% of world's population living in its territory.

Which one of the following is correct in respect of the above statements?

(a) Both Statement-I and Statement-II are correct, and Statement-II is the correct explanation for Statement-I

(b) Both Statement-I and Statement-II are correct, and Statement-II is not the correct explanation for Statement-I

(c) Statement-I is correct but Statement-II is incorrect

(d) Statement-I is incorrect but Statement-II is correct

97. Consider the following statements:

1. According to the Constitution of India, the Central Government has a duty to protect States from internal disturbances.
2. The Constitution of India exempts the States from providing legal counsel to a person being held for preventive detention.
3. According the Prevention of Terrorism Act, 2002, confession of the accused before the police cannot be used as evidence.

How many of the above statements are correct?

(a) Only one (b) Only two

(c) All three (d) None

98. Consider the following statements:

1. In India, the Biodiversity Management Committees are key to the realization of the objectives of the Nagoya Protocol.
2. The Biodiversity Management Committees have important functions in determining access and benefit sharing, including the power to levy collection fees on the access of biological resources within its jurisdiction.

Which of the statements given above is/are correct?

(a) 1 only (b) 2 only

(c) Both 1 and 2 (d) Neither 1 nor 2

99. Which one of the following countries has been suffering from decades of civil strife and food shortages and was in news in the recent past for its very severe famine?

(a) Angola (b) Costa Rica

(c) Ecuador (d) Somalia

100. Consider the following statements in respect of election to the President of India:

1. The members nominated to either House of the Parliament or the Legislative Assemblies of States are also eligible to be included in the Electoral College.
2. Higher the number of elective Assembly seats, higher is the value of vote of each MLA of that State.
3. The value of vote of each MLA of Madhya Pradesh is greater than that of Kerala.
4. The value of vote of each MLA of Puducherry is higher than that of Arunachal Pradesh because the ratio of total population to total number of elective seats in Puducherry is greater as compared to Arunachal Pradesh.

How many of the above statements are correct?

(a) Only one (b) Only two

(c) Only three (d) All four

UPSC CSE MAINS 2023 QUESTION PAPERS

GENERAL STUDIES (PAPER-I)

Time Allowed: Three Hours **Maximum Marks: 250**

Question Paper specific Instructions

(Please read each of the following instructions carefully before attempting questions)

- *There are TWENTY questions printed both in HINDI and in ENGLISH.*
- *All questions are compulsory.*
- *The Number of marks carried by a question/part is indicated against it.*
- *Answers must be written in the medium authorized in the Admission Certificate which must be stated clearly on the cover of this Questions-cum-Answer (QCA) Booklet in the space provided. No marks will be given for answers written in a medium other than the authorized one.*
- *Answers to Question Nos. 1 to 10 should be in 150 words each, whereas answers to Question Nos. 11 to 20 should be in 250 words each.*
- *Keep the word limit indicated in the questions in mind.*
- *Any page of portion of the page left blank in the Question-cum-Answer Booklet must be clearly struck off.*

1. Explain the role of geographical factors towards the development of Ancient India. 10
2. What was the difference between Mahatma Gandhi and Rabindranath Tagore in their approach towards education and nationalism? 10
3. Bring out the socio-economic effects of the introduction of railways in different countries of the world. 10
4. Discuss the consequences of climate change on the food security in tropical countries. 10
5. Why is the world today confronted with a crisis of availability of and access to freshwater resources? 10
6. How are the fjords formed? Why do they constitute some of the most picturesque areas of the world? 10
7. Why is the South-West Monsoon called 'Purvaiya' (easterly) in Bhojpur Region? How has this directional seasonal wind system influenced the cultural ethos of the region? 10

8. Do you think marriage as sacrament is loosing its value in Modern India? 10
9. Explain why suicide among young women is increasing in Indian society. 10
10. Child cuddling is now being replaced by mobile phones. Discuss its impact on the socialization of children. 10
11. What are the main features of Vedic society and religion? Do you think some of the features are still prevailing in Indian society? 15
12. What were the major technological changes introduced during the Sultanate period? How did those technological changes influence the Indian society? 15
13. How did the colonial rule affect the tribals in India and what was the tribal response to the colonial oppression? 15
14. Comment on the resource potentials of the long coastline of India and highlight the status of natural hazard preparedness in these areas. 15
15. Identify and discuss the factors responsible for diversity of natural vegetation in India. Assess the significance of wildlife sanctuaries in rain forest regions of India. 15
16. Why did human development fail to keep pace with economic development in India? 15
17. From being net food importer in 1960s, India has emerged as a net food exporter to the world. Provide reasons. 15
18. Does urbanization lead to more segregation and/or marginalization of the poor in Indian metropolises? 15
19. Why is caste identity in India both fluid and static? 15
20. Discuss the impact of post-liberal economy on ethnic identity and communalism. 15

GENERAL STUDIES (PAPER-II)

1. "Constitutionally guaranteed judicial independence is a prerequisite of democracy." Comment. 10
2. Who are entitled to receive free legal aid? Assess the role of the National Legal Services Authority (NALSA) in rendering free legal aid in India. 10
3. "The states in India seem reluctant to empower urban local bodies both functionally as well as financially." Comment. 10
4. Compare and contrast the British and Indian approaches to Parliamentary sovereignty. 10
5. Discuss the role of Presiding Officers of state legislatures in maintaining order and impartiality in conducting legislative work and in facilitating best democratic practices. 10
6. The crucial aspect of development process has been the inadequate attention paid to Human Resource Development in India. Suggest measures that can address this inadequacy. 10
7. Discuss the role of the Competition Commission of India in containing the abuse of dominant position by the Multi-National Corporations in India. Refer to the recent decisions. 10
8. e-governance, as a critical tool of governance, has ushered in effectiveness, transparency and accountability in governments. What Inadequacies hamper the enhancement of these features? 10
9. 'Virus of Conflict is affecting the functioning of the SCO' In the light of the above statement point out the role of India in mitigating the problems. 10
10. Indian diaspora has scaled new heights in the West. Describe its economic and political benefits for India. 10
11. "The Constitution of India is a living instrument with capabilities of enormous dynamism. It is a constitution made for a progressive society." Illustrate with special reference to the expanding horizons of the right to life and personal liberty. 15
12. Explain the constitutional perspectives of Gender Justice with the help of relevant Constitutional Provisions and case laws. 15

13. Account for the legal and political factors responsible for the reduced frequency of using Article 356 by the Union Governments since mid 1990s. 15
14. Discuss the contribution of civil society groups for women's effective and meaningful participation and representation in state legislatures in India. 15
15. Explain the significance of the 101st Constitutional Amendment Act. To what extent does it reflect the accommodative spirit of federalism? 15
16. Explain the structure of the Parliamentary Committee system. How far have the financial committees helped in the institutionalisation of Indian Parliament? 15
17. "Development and welfare schemes for the vulnerable, by its nature, are discriminatory in approach." Do you agree? Give reasons for your answer. 15
18. Skill development programmes have succeeded in increasing human resources supply to various sectors. In the context of the statement analyse the linkages between education, skill and employment. 15
19. 'The expansion and strengthening of NATO and stronger US-Europe strategic partnership works well for India.' 15

    What is your opinion about this statement? Give reasons and examples to support your answer.
20. 'Sea is an important Component of the Cosmos' 15

    Discus in the light of the above statement the role of the IMO (International Maritime Organisation) in protecting environment and enhancing maritime safety and security.

GENERAL STUDIES (PAPER-III)

1. Faster economic growth requires increased share of the manufacturing sector in GDP, particularly of MSMEs. Comment on the present policies of the Government in this regard. 10
2. What is the status of digitalization in the Indian economy? Examine the problems faced in this regard and suggest improvements. 10
3. How dose e-Technology help farmers in production and marketing of agricultural produce? Explain it. 10
4. State the objectives and measures of land reforms in India. Discuss how land ceiling policy on landholding can be considered as an effective reform under economic criteria. 10
5. Introduce the concept of Artificial Intelligence (AI). How does AI help clinical diagnosis? Do you perceive any threat to privacy of the individual in the use of AI in healthcare? 10
6. Discuss several ways in which microorganisms can help in meeting the current fuel shortage. 10
7. Dam failures are always catastrophic, especially on the downstream side, resulting in a colossal loss of life and property. Analyze the various causes of dam failures. Give two examples of large dam failures. 10
8. What is oil pollution? What are its impacts on the marine ecosystem? In what way is oil pollution particularly harmful for a country like India? 10
9. Winning of 'Hearts and Minds' in terrorism-affected areas is an essential step in restoring the trust of the population. Discuss the measures adopted by the Government in this respect as part of the conflict resolution in Jammu and Kashmir. 10
10. The use of unmanned aerial vehicles (UAVs) by our adversaries across the borders to ferry arms/ammunitions, drugs,etc., is a serious threat to the internal security. Comment on the measures being taken to tackle this threat. 10
11. Most of the unemployment in India is structural in nature. Examine the methodology adopted to compute unemployment in the country and suggest improvements. 15
12. Distinguish between 'care economy' and 'monetized economy'. How can care economy be brought into monetized economy through women empowerment? 15

13. Explain the changes in cropping pattern in India in the context of changes in consumption pattern and marketing conditions. 15
14. What are the direct and indirect subsidies provided to farm sector in India? Discuss the issues raised by the World Trade Organization (WTO) in relation to agricultural subsidies. 15
15. The adoption of electric vehicles is rapidly growing worldwide. How do electric vehicles contribute to reducing carbon emissions and what are the key benefits they offer compared to traditional combustion engine vehicles? 15
16. What is the main task of India's third moon mission which could not be achieved in its earlier mission? List the countries that have achieved this task. Introduce the subsystems in the spacecraft launched and explain the role of the 'Virtual Launch Control Centre' at the Vikram Sarabhai Space Centre which contributed to the successful launch from Sriharikota. 15
17. Comment on the National Wetland Conservation Programme initiated by the Government of India and name a few India's wetlands of international importance included in the Ramsar Sites. 15
18. The Intergovernmental panel on Climate Change (IPCC) has predicted a global sea level rise of about one metre by AD 2100. What would be its impact in India and the other countries in the India Ocean region? 15
19. What are the internal security challenges being faced by India? Give out the role of Central Intelligence and Investigative Agencies tasked to counter such threats. 15
20. Give out the major sources of terror funding in India and the efforts being made to curtail these sources. In the light of this, also discuss the aim and objective of the 'No Money for Terror (NMFT)' Conference recently held at New Delhi in November 2022. 15

GENERAL STUDIES (PAPER-IV)

1. (a) What do you understand by 'moral integrity' and 'professional efficiency' in the context of corporate governance in India? Illustrate with suitable examples. 10

   (b) 'International aid' is an accepted form of helping 'resource-challenged' nations. Comment on 'ethics in contemporary international aid'. Support your answer with suitable examples. 10

2. (a) "Corruption is the manifestation of the failure of core value in the society." In your opinion, what measures can be adopted to uplift the core values in the society? 10

   (b) In the context of work environment, differentiate between 'coercion' and 'undue influence' with suitable examples. 10

3. (a) "The simplest acts of kindness are by far more powerful than a thousand heads bowing in prayer." – Mahatma Gandhi 10

   (b) "To awaken the people, it is the women who must be awakened. Once she is on the move, the family moves, the village moves, the nation moves." – Jawaharlal Nehru 10

   (c) "Do not hate anybody, because that hatred that comes out from you must, in the long run, come back to you. If you love, that love will come back to you, completing the circle." –Swami Vivekananda 10

4. (a) "What really matters for success, character, happiness and lifelong achievements is a definite set of emotional skills – your EQ – not just purely cognitive abilities that are measured by conventional IQ tests." Do you agree with this view? Give reasons in support of your answer. 10

   (b) Differentiate 'moral intuition' from 'moral reasoning' with suitable examples. 10

5. (a) Is conscience a more reliable guide when compared to laws, rules and regulations in the context of ethical decision-making? Discuss. 10

   (b) 'Probity is essential for an effective system of governance and socio-economic development.' Discuss. 10

6. (a) What were the major teachings of Guru Nanak? Explain their relevance in the contemporary world. 10

   (b) Explain the term social capital. How does it enhance good governance? 10

7. A few weeks later, you ask her about the well-being of her about the well-being of her father and she Informs you about his successful surgery and that he is

recovering. She then confides in you that the bank manager was kind enough to facilitate the release of Rs. 10 lakh from a dormant account of someone to pay for the operation with a promise that it should be confidential and be repaid at the earliest. She has already started paying it back and will continue to do so until it is all returned.

(a) What are the ethical issues involved?

(b) Evaluate the behaviour of the bank manager from an ethical point of view.

(c) How would you react to the situation? 20

8. A landslide occurred in the middle of the night on 20th July, 2023 in a remote mountain hamlet, approximately 60 kilometres from Uttarkashi. The landslide was caused by torrential rains and has resulted in large-scale destruction of property and life. You, as District Magistrate of that area, have rushed to the spot with a team of doctors, NGOs, media and police along with numerous support staff to oversee the rescue operations.

   A man came running to you with a request for urgent medical help for his pregnant wife who is in labour and is losing blood. You directed your medical team to examine his wife. They return and convey to you that this woman needs blood transfusion immediately. Upon enquiry, you come to know that a few blood collection bags and blood group test kits are available in the ambulance accompanying your team. Few people of your team have already volunteered to donate blood.

   Being a physician who has graduated from AIIMS, you know hat blood for transfusion needs to be procured only through a recognized blood bank. Your team members are divided on this issue; some favour transfusion, while some others oppose it. The doctors in the team are ready to facilitate the delivery provided they are not penalized for transfusion. Now you are in a dilemma. Your professional training emphasizes on prioritising service to humanity and saving lives of individuals.

   (a) What are the ethical issues involved in this case?

   (b) Evaluate the options available to you, being District Magistrate of the area.

9. At 9 pm on Saturday evening, Rashika, a Joint Secretary, was still engrossed in her work in her office. Her husband, Vikram, is an executive in an MNC and frequently out of town in connection with his work. Their two children aged 5 and 3 are looked after by their domestic helper. At 9:30 pm her superior, Mr. Suresh calls her and asks her to prepare a detailed note on an important matter to be discussed in a meeting in the Ministry. She realises that she will have to work on Sunday to finish the additional task given by her superior.

She reflects on how she had looked forward to this posting and had worked long hours for months to achieve it. She had kept the welfare of people uppermost in discharging her duties. She feels that she has not done enough justice to her family and she has not fulfilled her duties in discharging essential social obligations. Even as recently as last month she had to leave her sick child in the nanny's care as she had to work in the office. Now, she feels that she must draw a line, beyond which her personal life should take precedence over her professional responsibilities. She thinks there should be reasonable limits to the work ethics such as punctuality, hard work, dedication to duty and selfless service.

(a) Discuss the ethical issues involved in this case.

(b) Briefly describe at least four laws that have been enacted by the Government with respect to providing a healthy, safe and equitable working environment for women.

(c) Imagine you are in a similar situation. What suggestions would you make to mitigate such working conditions? 20

10. Vinod is an honest and sincere IAS officer. Recently, he has taken over as Managing Director of the State Road Transport Corporation, his sixth transfer in the past three years. His peers acknowledge his vast knowledge, affability and uprightness. The Chairman of the State road Transport Corporation is a powerful politician and is very close to the Chief Minister. Vinod comes to know about many alleged irregularities of the Corporation and the high-handedness of the Chairman in financial matters.

A Board Member of the Corporation belonging to the Opposition Party meets Vinod and hands over a few documents along with a video recording in which the Chairman appears to be demanding bribe for placing a huge order for the supply of QMR tyres. Vinod recollects the Chairman expediting clearing of pending bills of QMR tyres.

Vinod confronts the Board Member as to why he is shying away from exposing the Chairman with the so-called solid proof he has with him. The member informs him that the Chairman refuses to yield to his threats. He adds that Vinod may earn recognition and public support if he himself exposes the Chairman. Further, he tell Vinod that one his party comes to power, Vinod's professional growth would be assured.

Vinod is aware that he may be penalized if he exposes the Chairman and may further be transferred to a distant place. He knows that the Opposition Party stands a better chance of coming to power in the forthcoming elections. However, he also realizes that the Board Member is trying to use him for his own political gains.

(a) As a conscientious civil servant, evaluate the options available to Vinod.

(b) In the light of the above case, comment upon the ethical issues that may arise due to the politicization of bureaucracy.

11. You have been appointed as Additional Director General of Central Public Works Department. The Chief Architect of your division, who is to retire in six months, is passionately working on a very important project, the successful completion of which would earn him a lasting reputation for the rest of his life.

A new lady architect, Seema, trained at Manchester, School of Architecture, UK joined as Senior Architect in your division. During the briefing about the project, Seema made some suggestions which would not only add value to the project, but would also reduce completion time. This has made the Chief Architect insecure and he is constantly worried that all the credit will go to her. Subsequently, he adopted a passive and aggressive behaviour towards her and has become disrespectful to her. Seema felt it embarrassing as the chief Architect left no chance of humiliating her. He would very often correct her in front of other colleagues and raise his voice while speaking to her. This continuous harassment has resulted in her losing confidence and self-esteem. She felt perpetually tensed, anxious and stressed. She appeared to be in awe of him since he has had long tenure in the office and has vast experience in the area of her work.

You are aware of her outstanding academic credentials and career record in her previous organisations. However, you fear that this harassment may result in compromising her much needed contribution in this important project and may adversely impact her emotional well-being. You have also come to know from her peers that she is contemplating tendering her resignation.

(a) What are the ethical issues involved in the above case?

(b) What are the options available to you in order to complete the project as well as to retain Seema in the organization?

(c) What would be your response to Seema's predicament? What measures would you institute to prevent such occurrences from happening in your organization?

12. You hold a responsible position in a ministry in the government. One day in the morning you received a call from the school of your 11-year-old son that you are required to come and meet the Principal. You proceed to the school and find your son in the Principal's office. The Principal informs you that your son had been found wandering aimlessly in the grounds during the time classes

were in progress. The class teacher further informs you that your son has lately become a loner and did not respond to questions in the class, he had also been unable to perform well in the football trials held recently. You bring your son back from the school and in the evening, you along with your wife try to find out the reasons for your son's changed behaviour. After repeated cajoling, your son shares that some children had been making fun of him in the class as well as in the WhatsApp group of the students by calling him stunted, duh and a frog. He tells you the names of a few children who are the main culprits but pleads with you to let the matter rest.

After a few days, during a sporting event, where you and your wife have gone to watch your son play, one of your colleague's son shows you a video in which students have caricatured your son. Further, he also points out to the perpetrators who were sitting in the stands. You purposefully walk past them with your son and go home. Next day, you find on social media, a video denigrating you, your son and even your wife, stating that you engaged in physical bullying of children on the sports field. The video became viral on social media. Your friends and colleagues began calling you to find out the details. One of your juniors advised you to make a counter video giving the background and explaining that nothing had happened on the field. You, in turn posted a video which you have captured during the sporting event, identifying the likely perpetrators who were responsible for your son's predicament. You have also narrated what has actually happened in the field and made attempts to bring out the adverse effects of the misuse of social media.

(a) Based on the above case study, discuss the ethical issues involved in the use of social media.

(b) Discuss the pros and cons of using social media by you to put across the facts to counter the fake propaganda against your family.

Essay

Time Allowed: Three Hours **Maximum Marks: 250**

Question Paper specific Instructions

(Please read each of the following instructions carefully before attempting questions)

- *The ESSAY must be written in the medium outhorized in the Admission Certificate which must be stated clearly on the cover of this Question-cum-Answer (QCA) Booklet in the space provided. No marks will be given for answers written in a medium other than the outhorized one.*
- *Word limit, as specified, should be adhered to.*
- *Any page or portion of the page left blank in the Question-cum-Answer (QCA) Booklet must be clearly struck off.*

Write two essays, choosing one topic from each of the following Sections A and B, in about 1000-1200 words each: 125×2 = 250

Section A

1. Thinking is like a game, it does not being unless there is an opposite team.
2. Visionary decision-making happens at the intersection of intuition and logic.
3. Not all who wander are lost.
4. Inspiration for creativity springs from the effort to look for the magical in the mundane.

Section B

5. Girls are weighed down by restrictions boys with demands – two equally harmful disciplines.
6. Mathematics is the music of reason.
7. A society that has more justice is a society that needs less charity.
8. Education is what remains after one has forgotten what one has learned in school.